This was the most extraordinary mission of the entire Cold War—led and finally told by the most unassuming hero. Over the four decades of the struggle with the Soviet Union, hundreds of submarine commanders sailed into the teeth of Russia's defenses. Their goal was to keep the Soviets on their heels. A dozen of the particularly successful men were selected to return to the White House to personally brief the President of the United States. But of those, only Dave Minton could tell the story of alerting the president of a nuclear threat to America, protecting three aircraft carriers, also altering the Vietnam War, and ...

— Rear Adm. David Oliver, U.S. Navy (Ret.)

Dave has written an accurate account of our pressure-packed operation of the trail of a Russian ECHO class submarine. Once we realized that this movement of five submarines without prior knowledge was of interest at the highest levels of our government, every minute was filled with excitement and fear that we would lose contact. Every member of the crew did his part in keeping Guardfish capable of finishing the job without failure.

— Rear Adm. Larry G. Vogt U.S. Navy (Ret.), former executive officer, USS Guardfish (SSN612)

FROM
OPPOSITE SIDES
OF THE
PERISCOPE

FROM
OPPOSITE SIDES
OF THE
PERISCOPE

The Trail Is On

**Capt. David C. Minton III USN (Ret.) *and*
Rear Adm. Alfred S. Berzin USSR (Ret.)**

ARCHWAY
PUBLISHING

Archway Publishing books may be ordered through booksellers or by contacting:

Archway Publishing
1663 Liberty Drive
Bloomington, IN 47403
www.archwaypublishing.com
1 (888) 242-5904

ISBN: 978-1-4808-5555-7 (sc)
ISBN: 978-1-4808-5553-3 (hc)
ISBN: 978-1-4808-5554-0 (e)

Library of Congress Control Number: 2017918982

Print information available on the last page.

Archway Publishing rev. date: 04/02/2018

PREFACE

The spring of 1972 *was* a very perilous time. For not only was war raging in Indochina, a second war, a Cold War, raged in secret as well. The question, without an answer, was would the bombing and mining campaigns of the Hanoi and Haiphong harbors, announced by President Nixon on May 8, 1972, bring the two superpowers into a violent collision? Would the presence of nuclear submarines, both Soviet and U.S., turn the Cold War hot?

It was during several weeks in 1972 that one lone nuclear submarine prevented the tactical morass of the Vietnam War from engulfing the strategic success of our Cold War containment. This submarine, USS *Guardfish* (SSN 612) commanded by Commander David C. Minton III, was the only source of hard intelligence available to our government and provided real time tactical information on the Soviet submarine threat to our carrier forces which were operating off Vietnam. Our carriers were deploying thousands of sorties into North and South Vietnam. Under this tremendous operational burden they were especially vulnerable to attack.

Sending U.S. submarines to protect the carrier groups engendered a big risk. No one knew how much Moscow knew about what was going on in the South China Sea. It seemed unreasonable that the Soviets would deploy their nuclear submarines to the South China Sea armed with nuclear missiles in response to the new U.S. mining and bombing policy, but they did. The presence of so many forces in close proximity could lead to an error in judgement or missed communication resulting in a catastrophic conflict.

The U.S. submarines would need to prevent the Soviet submarines from coming into missile range of our carrier groups, while the carriers continued prosecuting the air war in Vietnam. Yet it was only one U.S. submarine trailing a Soviet nuclear submarine that was in a position to alert our naval forces when the Soviets were closing into missile range. It was not originally supposed to be this way. *Guardfish*, had been stationed in the Sea of Japan outside of Vladivostok, was not involved in the Vietnam War, but was the tip of the spear in the Pacific Cold War. Its orders were to be on the lookout for any significant deployment of Soviet submarines from the port – perhaps a clue that the Soviets had changed their minds about not getting involved.

This is the story of the USS *Guardfish* (SSN 612) trail of the Soviet Guided Missile Submarine K 184, from Vladivostok to the South China Sea, in the wake of the mining of the Haiphong and Hanoi harbors during the Vietnam War. It is the true story of a twenty-eight day, six thousand one hundred nautical mile covert trail conducted during the summer of 1972. It is also the intertwined story of two men, young commanders, whose lives were very different, but whose careers paralleled that of the other in a surprisingly intimate manner – their schooling, their training, the upward trajectory to command, finally converging in the waters just beyond the USSR's main deep water military port in the Pacific

There are always men on the eyepiece of the other periscope, but the stories of both of these adversaries together are rare. So too is the declassification of material needed to tell such tales.[1] All of these come together here.

Here are the two adversaries in dress uniforms, not the working uniforms typical used during patrol operations.

---

[1] A copy of the declassification document is contained in Chapter X.

Commander David C. Minton III, USN in 1972

Soviet Captain First Rank Alfred Berzin in 1972 [2]

---

[2] Appendix C compares the U.S. naval officer ranks with their Soviet counter parts.

DEDICATION

This book is dedicated to U.S. and Soviet submariners who went to sea during the Cold War. They competed in a dangerous chess game of surveillance while walking a fine line between war and peace. The sole objective was a stalemate while testing each other's strengths and weaknesses.

Submariners went beneath the sea for long periods in magnificently complex machines which demanded the utmost of the officers and crews. Submarines of that era were not as capable as today's boats. Therefore many shipboard functions depended solely on the professionalism and intense focus of the crew. Work hours were longer and there was little time for relaxation or diversion. Additionally the officers and crew were away from their families and loved ones for much of their naval career. This separation weighed heavily on the men, as it did on their families.

During the Cold War there were many serious accidents and a number of deadly collisions resulting in loss of life. It was a dangerous occupation, but a necessity of those tense times where our two governments jockeyed for power and dominance.

Despite the tension, submariners on both sides were thankful that no shots were fired and the long conflict ended in PEACE.

TABLE OF CONTENTS

TABLE OF FIGURES AND PHOTOS

THE TRAIL

WASHINGTON D.C., USA

And so it began, like so many others things, an unanticipated consequence of a decision made halfway around the world. In the hopes of forcing the North Vietnamese back to the table after the secret Paris Peace talks with North Vietnam had broken down, the U.S. government decided to deny the North Vietnamese the advantage of readily receiving supplies from their communist allies in the Soviet Union, China, and North Korea through the port of Haiphong and other major North Vietnamese harbors. At 10:00 p.m. on May 8, 1972 — because of the International Date Line it was May 9 in Vietnam — President Nixon announced the mining of Hanoi and Haiphong harbors and a policy of intensifying the bombing of North Vietnamese military targets. Because roughly 85 percent of North Vietnam's imports came through Haiphong, Nixon already had directed supply ships destined for the Haiphong harbor to be followed by U.S. submarines assigned to the Seventh Fleet. Now he would go farther. He would, over the course of the campaign, drop more than eleven thousand mines in North Vietnamese coastal waters. He would close Haiphong harbor for three hundred days.

The President hoped that this new initiative would drive the North Vietnamese to agree to an internationally supervised cease-fire throughout Indochina and that such a cease fire might lead to the return of all Americans, including all POWs. Defending his actions — the escalation of the bombing and the denial of shipboard materials entering the mined harbors, Nixon hoped such pressure would bring the North Vietnamese back to the talks. In Nixon's announcement to the American people, he said:

> "I have ordered the following measures, which are being implemented as I am speaking to you. All entrances to North Vietnamese ports will be mined to prevent access to these ports and North Vietnamese naval operations from these ports. United States forces have been directed to take appropriate measures within the international and claimed territorial waters of North Vietnam to interdict the delivery of supplies. Rail and all communications will be cut off to the maximum extent possible. Air and Naval strikes against North Vietnam will continue." [3]

There were many unknowns. The North Vietnamese had endured catastrophic losses over the course of the war. Would this be enough to bring the war to a close? Or would the North Vietnamese persevere? Were their inland supply routes sufficient for them to hold out? What were the ramifications to ships already in the harbor? They would be trapped. What would this do to the harbor long term? After the war was over — and surely it would be soon — Haiphong harbor needed to be viable. And finally, what of North Vietnam's communist allies? That was most worrisome. Would this jeopardize the new U.S. – China relationship? And more importantly, how would the USSR react to America's escalation? More specifically — more vitally — would they send a naval response of their own?

President Nixon's use of coercive diplomacy — "the use of military power, or threat of its use, to modify an adversary's behavior" — was perilous because of possible retributory escalation by the nuclear-armed Soviet Union and the Chinese. To mitigate such an effect, on May 3, 1972, the United States reached out to Leonid Brezhnev

---

[3] Department of the Navy and John Sherwood, *Nixon's Trident: Naval Power in Southeast Asia 1968–1972, (the U.S. Navy and the Vietnam War)*, (Create Space Independent Publishing Platform, 2013), 87.

and the Chinese, informing them of our intent. While both expressed strong reservations, their diplomatic responses suggested that they themselves would not escalate. But such a response was ambiguous. The U.S. Navy, already on a war footing, would go to extra lengths, monitoring the sea lanes not for supply ships alone but also for the movement of Chinese forces and more dangerously, a pronounced naval military presence streaming out of Russian ports.

VLADIVOSTOK, RUSSIA [4]

On the Soviet submarine base orders had arrived. On May 9, 1972, I was handed the following intelligence summary:

> *"In the area of the Indo-China Peninsula, combat action has been carried out against the patriotic forces of Indo-China for the Tonkin Gulf (130 miles to the north of Da Nang) by the strike carriers Coral Sea, Kitty Hawk, and Saratoga; and from an area 170 miles to the southeast of Saigon the strike carrier Constellation with thirty-eight ships in support. The carriers launched 353 sorties, 256 of them strike sorties."*

The Americans had attacked our Vietnamese brothers and we were being called to strike back. Brezhnev responded to the American escalation. In the second half of the day, the Soviet Pacific Fleet went to a higher state of readiness and our submarines sounded general quarters. All crews were required to return to their ships immediately. The mood of the day was somber but determined. Once on board, preparations were undertaken for the long cruise. In addition to the submarine I commanded, Echo II SSGN K 184, we would be accompanied by

---

[4] In order to distinguish between Captain Minton's and Admiral Berzin's narratives Admiral Berzin's narrative is printed in italics.

four other nuclear submarines, including one that was deploying from Petropavlovsk on the Kamchatka Peninsula.[5]

Vladivostok was the Soviet Navy's largest port in the Pacific. Ice free all year around, it was the home of the Soviet Pacific Fleet. As Commanding Officer, I was in charge of an Echo II class anti-carrier submarine, with a crew of one hundred nine and armed with eight Shaddock missiles, four of them nuclear, four of them conventional. The ship was designed to launch cruise missiles from the surface.

Over the course of May 9, preparations for imminent deployment were carried out. There was immediacy to all our actions although we still did not know what specifically the mission was to be. Espionage? Tracking? Would we engage? We believed American ships carried nuclear weapons much as our own did. Would the American President be crazy enough to use them?

Yet such questions did not affect the primary objective that faced me now — get K 184 away from the pier and into deep waters.

By the morning of May 10, both reactors were brought online to the turbo generators. Nuclear reactors need a lengthy starting time, perhaps twelve hours to self-sustaining readiness. Orders were given to conduct the pre-critical safety testing of the reactor instrumentation, to pull the control rods to bring both reactor plants to criticality followed by heating up of the secondary plant and lighting off of the turbo-generators. Once the submarine's electrical systems were powered by our own generators, shore power cables would be disconnected.

Our combat orders came in the form of a telegraph. We were to head into the Sea of Japan and transit south — under strict silence. I received my final instructions from the Division Commander, determined that K 184 was at full readiness, and then we slipped silently away.

---

[5] *The submarines following behind us from Vladivostok were Echo I SSGN K 45 (Captain 1ˢᵗ Rank Yu.N. Ganzha, commanding), Echo II SSGN K 57(Captain 1ˢᵗ Rank Yu.F. Shipovnikov, commanding), Echo II SSGN K 189, and Echo II SSGN K 7 deploying from Petropavlovsk on the Kamchatka Peninsula.*

SEA OF JAPAN

On May 9 I received a message from the Commander of the Seventh Fleet, my operational commander, to be alert for a possible Soviet naval response to the mining of North Vietnamese ports.

On *Guardfish*, patrolling close to the Vladivostok Soviet naval base, the situation was tense. No one knew what the USSR's reaction would be. I brought the submarine at periscope depth close to the line that marked the international boundary to Soviet waters.

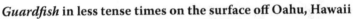

Guardfish in less tense times on the surface off Oahu, Hawaii

Guardfish waited just southwest of the main channel entrance to Vladivostok. On the approaches to the base, the Soviets had moored a number of large sonar buoys called twin cylinders because of their large cylindrical configuration. These buoys were designed to alert the shore command of an approaching ship and could be triggered by the sound of a ship's cavitating screws (propellers). Once triggered, the buoys transmitted the sounds to the Soviet base via radio. Because

U.S. submarines on covert operations never cavitated, the buoys were more of a collision hazard than anything else.

On the evening of May 10, our sonar detected a noise level from the northwest, in the direction of Askold Island. As it drew closer, the contact was initially classified by sonar as a patrol craft coming at high speed almost directly toward *Guardfish*. The Officer of the Deck, Lieutenant Richard C. Woodward, notified me of the contact and I directed him to call me when it had come into visual range. I was just finishing dinner when I was called to the control room. Looking through the periscope I could clearly see the contact's side lights. The starboard light was a yellowish green, a unique characteristic of Soviet submarines that I had seen many times before. Strangely, the contact was deviating from standard naval practice by leaving the marked channel. The reasons for this protocol were to avoid several Soviet exercise operating areas and to avoid the twin cylinders. Suddenly the Soviet submarine activated one of the twin cylinders guarding the base. Searching the seas in the growing darkness, I was able to make out four external starboard missile-launch cavities along its hull. We were being passed by a Soviet Echo II Class submarine.

This photo shows a Soviet Echo II submarine.
Note the eight missile launch cavities.

It was close, very close. We were lucky — we had remained un-detected and had been able to visually identify the submarine's class. We would not have to depend upon the submarine's sonar signature for identification. Knowledge of a contact's class was essential in any surveillance for it narrowed down the type of deployment he was conducting and his capability.

The Echo II class submarines displaced five thousand tons, were powered by two nuclear reactors, and carried eight Shaddock missiles that could be either conventional or nuclear. The Shaddock missiles were specifically designed to kill aircraft carriers. Not until forty years later would I learn that K 184 was armed with four nuclear missiles and two torpedoes with nuclear warheads. The effective range of the Shaddock was two hundred miles.

My operation orders did not specify that I follow any submarine that we located, only that we were to be on the lookout for a significant deployment of Soviet naval vessels. A single submarine leaving Vladivostok, albeit one with an unusual exit from the harbor, did not in my estimation constitute such an event. Nevertheless, as there was no other Soviet naval activity in the area — an oddity in and of itself — I ordered the Officer of the Deck to follow. When the submarine submerged, we went deep and started to follow her on her transit to the south at high speed. I still wasn't sure if this submarine was headed to Haiphong or was simply on a training mission in the Sea of Japan. Regardless, we would stay with her for a while and see where she took us.

Unbeknownst to me, I had just begun one of the longest trails in U.S. submarine history. Two nuclear powered subs, armed with ready weapons, one trailing the other deep below the surface of the sea, utterly blind but for our sonars. It is a story that would play out over the next twenty-eight days and worked its way into the lore of the United States Navy.

But the full story begins much earlier in a village outside of Moscow, in 1933.

CHAPTER I

РАННЕЕ ДЕТСТВО ЛЕТ

(Early Childhood Years)

Born on June 1, 1933, Alfred Simenovich Berzin came into the world loudly. He announced his arrival with a hearty cry so deep it caused the doctor attending to the birth to announce that he would be a ship's captain. And so he would first become a commander of a nuclear submarine, then a Rear Admiral commanding a division of nuclear submarines.

His birth came only seventeen years after the 1917 Revolution, which meant that he lived in the shadows of Czars and nobility. And it certainly meant he lived in tumult. During the summer of 1933 in Germany Hitler came to power. In the Soviet Union, a wave of 'arrests' of public enemies swept his country and Stalin became a dictator.

His was a small town, Rabochii, set upon a hill overlooking a small river. The houses were much the same, two stories and made of wood, and lined with plaster, both inside and out. Each home had one heating stove and an outhouse. The only water supplied to the house was cold water to the communal kitchen. The house was comprised of three single room apartments. Berzin's family — mother, grandmother, and Alfred — lived in one room. There were two beds, a dresser, and a black plate radio. There was a single window, and sunlight would filter through only late at night in the summertime when the sun was beginning to set.

It was an austere life shaped by poverty and hardship, one shared by millions of others throughout the Soviet Union. Yet, a boy can find endless adventures to occupy his time. Playing outside, young Alfred found spring to be a time for building small boats to float on the endless streams. April was the month the sap would run in the birch trees and he and his friends would tap the trees and sip the delicious syrup. In May, the month of May beetles, they would catch the flying insects by the dozens, gently placing them in boxes made from birch leaves, and then trade them back and forth, only setting them free in the evening. In the summer, the boys would venture into the forest, play in the meadows, and swim in the creek in the woods. In December, Alfred's mother would take her skis and head into the country and return with a large evergreen tree. That evening the family would gather and decorate the tree — a rarity at the time.

Alfred's grandmother played a formidable role in his life, as his mother worked out of the house to provide for their family. Grandmother Emma was Latvian. Alfred was Latvian by descent. She grew up in a small village called Palshi with her family of six, mother father and three siblings. Her father was prosperous at first, a gardener working for a 'Black Baron,' an affluent German absentee landlord. But assailed with drinking problems, he lost that job and took another position with a 'Gray Baron,' a Latvian farmer, less known for such generosity.

Emma's father raised his sons in a hard manner, flogging them for any misdemeanor. All became atheists. Emma and her middle brother, Carl, went on to become Bolsheviks, members of the Russian Social Democratic Labor Party. Later, Carl would be slandered and arrested. He ended up being shot during a period when there was an order to 'cleanse' the Latvian Bolsheviks. Alfred's uncle, also named Carl, was an Asaysargi. The Asaysargi was a nationalist paramilitary unit that, during the occupation of Latvia, carried out police and punitive actions ordered by the Nazis. In 1941, Carl was drafted into the Red Army and was sent to the Front, where he won a medal. Despite this, upon his return, he was accused of being an Asaysargi, was convicted, and sent to Magadan, the headquarters for the Gulag of northeastern Siberia, where he died.

This was the twentieth century, one of violence, blood, and assault. Russia and its republics lived in fear under the iron fist of Stalin, burdened by the endless struggle of poverty and the turbulence of a world on the brink of war. Yet, even as the hateful tentacles of chaos spread across the globe, a far distant scenario was playing out in the United States of America.

MINTON'S EARLY CHILDHOOD YEARS

Far from Moscow, I was born in Leavenworth, Kansas on November 20, 1934 (one year and five months after Rear Admiral Berzin's birth). My mother and father had been living in Mexico where my father was working as a mining engineer and a metallurgist. He was employed by a group of European investors to evaluate the viability of mines that had been abandoned during the depression. My dad and his foreman, Rubin Velasquez, managed a workforce of several hundred Mexican laborers to establish camps and the necessary facilities. As a result of a common practice of salting mines with small amounts of high grade ore to trick investors, it was necessary for the mines to be restarted to obtain representative samples of the mine's actual value.

At various mining camps my parents lived in crude accommodations including tents, shacks, and even an adobe house built for them by the workers.

Because of poor medical facilities in these remote areas my parents decided that it would be much safer to send my mother back to her mother's home in Kansas for my birth. Therefore I became a Kansan.

I was four years old when I first went to sea. My father had just been hired as the first director of the Mining Engineering Department of the newly established college, School of the Philippines, in Manila. In October of 1938, my first sea voyage was from San Francisco, California, to Manila on the SS *President Coolidge.* When the *Coolidge* was delivered to the Dollar Line in 1931, she was the largest passenger ship constructed in America. The name Dollar was the surname of the founder of this steamship line, not the price. A large dollar sign was painted on the ship's funnel.

I can remember how much I enjoyed being at sea and watching

the waves and the ship's white wake trailing off in the distance astern. It was quite a sight from the upper decks. On the ship was a group of young men on a fateful adventure of their own. They were going to China with Richard Halliburton to outfit and sail a Chinese junk from Hong Kong to San Francisco. They sort of adopted me and I remember being chased and lifted up to ride on their shoulders.

Richard Halliburton was well known at that time as an adventurer, an author, and world traveler. He visited exotic locales such as the Taj Mahal in India, climbed the Matterhorn, flew across the Sahara desert in a bi-winged plane, and he was the first person ever to swim the length of the Panama Canal. When asked to pay a toll for his passage, it was decided that he should pay the freight rate based on his weight, incurring a charge of thirty-six cents. He also roamed the Mediterranean Sea retracing the route followed by Ulysses in Homer's *Odyssey* and crossed the Swiss Alps on the back of an elephant in a recreation of Hannibal's expedition. Alas, the Chinese junk Halliburton captained was unseaworthy and went down in a storm around March 1939. Their bodies were never recovered.

During my family's stay in Manila, we lived right on Manila Bay in a gated community and in front of our home were several rusting hulks of Spanish ships sunk in the Spanish American War. When the tide was way out my dad would take me down on the beach so I could actually touch these old hulks. Because some of the hulks still had their propellers my dad took along a file to test if they were made of bronze or brass, unfortunately any propellers made of valuable metals were long gone. They made quite an impression on me. On the beach in front of our house grew a city of poor Filipino shacks. Every evening one of the men would climb up an electric pole and hook up an illegal jumper cable to light up the whole shanty town. The jumpers were quickly removed in the morning and any time the power company came around.

My young friends and I thought it was great fun to throw rocks over our fence and yell at the children across the road. It was the first time I saw such poverty and regret my action to this day.

One winter while we lived in Manila, we went on a Christmas sightseeing cruise through the southern Philippine Islands to Leyte,

Cebu, Mindanao, Zamboanga, and Borneo. Although I had a great time and was fascinated by the many fishing boats and small cargo ships, the only thing that really concerned me was, "How was Santa Claus going to find us here at sea and without a chimney?" My mom and dad assured me that Santa would find us and that he would come by boat. And sure enough he arrived right on time.

My parents made friends with a number of U.S. Naval Officers and their families in Manila and as a result were invited to visit several of the ships stationed there. One I remember was the Navy repair ship, USS *Blackburn*. While pretty old, it was a bustle of activity with big machine shops and a foundry. It was a great place for a little boy.

However, Manila, along with the rest of the South Pacific, was a soon to become a very dangerous place. The Japanese were gearing up for war, initially with the China and then with the World. In 1940 my dad had observed that the Japanese were buying scrap metal from all over the Pacific Rim, including the United States. On a business trip to Japan he was surprised that there were almost no metal objects on the market. Though the Americans were aware of such activities, they would be utterly surprised by the aggression of the Japanese.

Yet, a continent away, war already had come to the world. Months before the attack on Pearl Harbor and the invasion of the Philippine Islands, a devastating action was taking place that would eventually consume us all.

CHAPTER II

ЖИЗНЬ ВО ВРЕМЯ ВТОРОЙ МИРОВОЙ ВОЙНЫ

(Life in the Soviet Union during World War II)

On June 19, 1941, Alfred Berzin turned eight years old. Three days later, the war with Nazi Germany began.

Early in the morning people in the village of Rabochii were awakened by the sound of what they thought was thunder. Everyone got up and looked out the window and saw squadrons of German planes heading for Moscow. At noon on June 21, Soviet foreign minister Vyacheslav Molotov announced:

> "...Without a declaration of war, German forces on our country attacked frontiers in many places. . .The Red Army and the whole nation will wage a victorious Patriotic War for our beloved country, for honor, for liberty. Our cause is just. The enemy will be beaten. Victory will be ours."

And so began Operation Barbarossa, as the Germans made the catastrophic decision to open up a second front of WWII launching the largest German military operation of the war. With three million German soldiers, augmented by 650,000 troops from her allies, the invasion stretched from the Baltic Sea in the north to the Black Sea in the south, a 1,800 mile front. The bombing of Moscow commenced on the first day of the campaign and while the sorties did not reach the center of the city, they did reach outlying areas. It was reported the individual tanks broke through the lines at Khimki, a city in the Moscow district, just northwest of the central city, on the west bank of the Moscow Canal. The damage the Luftwaffe inflicted was devastating. By the end of the first week, they had achieved air supremacy and destroyed thousands of Soviet aircraft — the bulk of the force.

There they saw German warplanes flying towards Moscow beneath white clouds of bursting shells. The week before, the Telegraph Agency of the Soviet Union (TASS) had assured the entire population of the Soviet Union that "speculation" about a war with Germany was unsubstantiated. A day before the war started, Alfred's grandmother, while reading the newspaper, *Pravda*, said that war with Germany would not happen, but added: "I do not believe Hitler."

As they listened to the anti-aircraft fire, Berzin's mother hastily made breakfast and rushed to the factory where she worked. Everyone was worried and confused. It was announced that the factory would be working for the war effort. Near the factory's entrance a large map of the Soviet Union was hung. Every day flags marked the front line, but it was removed quickly, as the advancement of German troops had a depressing effect on the mood of the population. Soon the Moscow area, including Berzin's township, was surrounded by nests of anti-aircraft guns. Barrage balloons were silhouetted against the evening sky and trenches were dug around the nests.[6]

The Germans did not bomb Rabochii because the one factory only produced stockings and boots. But every time Moscow was attacked by air, the village's anti-aircraft guns came alive and fragments of shells rained down like hail.

---

[6] Barrage balloons were large balloons tethered with metal cables, used to defend against low-level aircraft attack by damaging the aircraft on collision with the cables, or at least making the attacker's approach more difficult.

Anti-Aircraft Gun near Alfred Berzin's Home

Elderly civilians and children were evacuated to the basement shelter of an unfinished house. An air-raid alert was declared by a siren which was installed on the fire tower. At this signal, the villagers would grab their ready bags, filled with necessary things, take the hands of the young children and rush to the shelter, often under the fall of red hot shrapnel.

Young boys would later gather these fragments and collect them. They were a visible trophy of the war.

A rationing system was introduced and immediately everyone — men, women, and children had to "tighten their belt" because there was no food reserve in case of war. Because of such shortages, the factory manager decided to send all of the children to summer in the village of Efremovka in the district of Yegoryevsky, away from the bombing. On September 1, 1941, Berzin began first grade at the village school; his grandmother began work in the kindergarten dining room, and his mother remained in Rabochii to work at the factory.

The United States was still out of the war, but in the USSR, the military situation was worsening. In late September, the Germans reached the gates of Leningrad. By mid-October, martial law had been declared in Moscow. By early December, the Germans' ground troops and tanks had reached the outskirts of the city. Many businesses were evacuated to the east, but the "Winning Work" to help the war effort remained in place.

By this time, German planes were flying directly over Efremovka, which lies to the east of Moscow, sometimes shooting at the herd of cows grazing in the communal field. Like many others, the Berzins did not have any money. Fortunately Alfred's teacher let them stay with her in a closed veranda, though it was not heated. They were reduced to begging for potato peelings from the collective farm, so as to make potato cakes. When winter came, the teacher allowed them to stay in her kitchen and sleep on the benches. One did what one had to survive. The front was very close. Day and night exploding shells and bombs could be heard, and even at night the sky in the west was lit with crimson flares. Everyone was greatly emaciated and the children's heads were covered with scabs from beriberi and lice. They were always hungry.

Sooner or later the bad always comes to an end, and finally spring came and then summer. The villagers went into the woods where they gathered a fantastic amount of mushrooms and filled their bellies.

Alfred's mother, who had moved on to Tuschino, a small village northwest of Moscow, sent for Alfred and her mother. She had been appointed a Chief Deputy of an evacuation hospital in Krasnogorsk. The front was still not far away and there were many wounded. His father, who left at the beginning of the war to join the war effort, volunteered with his younger brother to go to the Front, where they both were killed near Smolensk.

After a time, Alfred's mother left the hospital and took a job as editor of the factory newspaper, *Patriot*. As she was now fed at the factory's kitchen, she gave Alfred and his grandmother her coupons, so they could recover a little from the hungry months in the village of Efremovka. In the summer, Alfred was sent to a summer camp for nearly three months.

It is a wonder that this happened during the brutal battle with Nazi Germany. Years later Admiral Berzin would marvel that, yes, at that time the government was thinking about the younger generation. There they were fed well. Near the camp a defensive line was held. There were deep trenches and shelters which the Germans very nearly reached. A military instructor at the camp was an officer who had defended Moscow during the invasion. Though he had lost one arm and one eye, he initiated military exercises with the children. There was no time for boredom.

In 1944, Alfred's mother was sent to Latvia, to the city of Dvinsk, where she began working as an editor of the county newspaper. Yet the rest of the family stayed in the town of Krasnogorsk where throughout the war there was no fuel to heat the house. There, they were given two six meter long logs which were piled next to the house. He and his grandmother used a little saw to cut them. When fuel ran low, Alfred would go to a nearby forest to get dry twigs and the bark of old pines. He was ten years old.

Finally, a letter came from Mom in which she wrote.

Sunday, September 24, 1944

"Hello, my dear!

I'll start with how I arrived and settled here. I arrived yesterday morning having had to change trains three times. From Moscow to Velikie Luki, I rode in a passenger train, then from Velikie Luki to Nevel I traveled by freight car, then from Nevel to Polotsk by a platform train and finally from Polotsk to Dvinsk again by freight car.

I arrived in Dvinsk in the morning, said goodbye to the people I had been traveling with and hired a boy to carry luggage. I walked on Riga Street straight from the station to the center of the city. I found the location of my new job very quickly but had to wait because it was too early in the morning and there was nobody there. Then we prepared and signed all the necessary papers and I was offered to rest for a couple of days in Dvinsk before starting my job. I settled in a hostel, washed up, got dressed, had lunch, and despite the fatigue went to see the city. The town was severely destroyed. There are whole streets where all the houses were gone. This was all the result of German mines laid by the Nazis before they left the town. There were still fresh signs on some buildings and fences posted by our miners saying 'the house cleared' which means it is safe. Overall the entire city has been cleared of these tricks and now has a peaceful air. Despite the severe destruction, the city makes an excellent impression. All the houses are made of stone with beautiful architecture, the streets are straight and paved with stone, sidewalks are wide, paved, and the city is very clean everywhere. The Daugava River is beautiful but the bridge was blown up and gone. One can only cross the river by a pontoon bridge, like in Irkutsk. Obviously I will have to live here until spring.

Before the war people living here were very wealthy, as can be seen even now after three years of occupation. The Germans tried to steal everything and yet the people here do not look as bad off as in our town. Any piece of clothing, even the simplest, has the imprint of beauty and was made with good taste. The market trading is still weak.

My coworker showed me my apartment. The apartment is located in a detached house with three rooms and a kitchen. One of the rooms is occupied by the owner of the house, she lives alone. I took the second room and the third will stay empty in reserve. The kitchen is just like you are familiar with. It has a stove, a sink with hot water, an oven, and everything is lined with ceramic tiles. There is no furniture yet, but there will be an opportunity to get everything I need from the financial department manager who is in charge. Local residents, who left with the Germans (collaborators), took their furniture to the parish, where it can now be requisitioned. I think that over time we will be able to settle here very well, although nothing happens without difficulty. The main thing for me right now is my job. I need to organize all over again and earn credibility in this new location.

I forgot to write to you about the food here and I know you'll worry about it. There is a dining room, where they feed us three times a day, with meals that include bread. I do not know anything about my wages yet, but there should not be a big change. Soon I will come over and bring you here.

Sending you my hugs and kisses."

LIFE IN AMERICA DURING WORLD WAR II

In 1940, in America, there was growing concern about the intentions of Japan. Indeed, the ambitions of the Rising Sun had begun to concern the entire world. Japanese aggression in China caused great unease in the United States, Australia, and future Allied Powers who still had colonial interests in Asia. President Roosevelt committed economic and military support to China, and the War and Navy departments quietly began updating and revising their amphibious landing protocols and training. Many of the Americans living in Manila and in the Philippines Islands, including my mother and father, felt the unease as well and began making preparations to leave and return home to the United States. It was a strange period among the expats living in the Philippines. Many had successful businesses in the Islands, others were from other countries including Germany, and some felt that staying through the Japanese occupation would not be too difficult.

Yet, despite many warnings, and the actions of the War and Navy departments, our government, still unsure of Japanese intent, delayed preparing for war. In the resulting confusion, military transport ships were bringing in U.S. army families while evacuating navy dependents (families) on their return trips. My father decided to send my mom and me home to the United States along with our car, a 1934 Hupmobile. He felt obligated to stay and finish teaching an accelerated mining engineering course for as many of his students as possible. We left on a small copra ship with five or six passenger staterooms. Copra is the dried meat, or kernel, of the coconut. Coconut oil extracted from it made copra an important agricultural commodity for many coconut producing countries. It also yields coconut "cake" which is mainly used as feed for livestock.

For a couple of weeks, the ship sailed from one small island to another small island to load copra. The process worried my mom because at each island they would lift up our car from the cargo hold and set it on the pier. Once they had the car on the pier, copra was loaded into the hold. The car was then placed back on top of that load and so it went.

Once the cargo hold was full, the ship headed for California. With passage across the Pacific Ocean in high demand, the staterooms were doubled up and in our room was a young lady, a professional softball player whose team had been playing all around Asia. She liked to stay up late playing music and it became obvious that I was not going to get the sleep a young boy needed. My mother went to the Captain and asked for another sleeping arrangement. Unfortunately there was no extra space, but the Mess Steward offered to give up his stateroom and sleep with the crew. Although very generous of him, there was still a problem. He had two pet squirrels living on the ceiling pipes and my mother was frightened by them. The Chief Engineer and I had become great friends and on hearing of our problem he solved it by tossing the squirrels overboard.

Several days into our transpacific passage we encountered a large typhoon. The seas were fifty to sixty feet high, the winds howling like mad. It was so rough, no meals were served for several days and the ship was buttoned up tight. All of the passengers and most of the crew were seasick except for my mother and me. It is fortunate for us that we never got seasick and it never occurred to me to be scared because my mother took everything in stride. After three days, she and I decided to raid the pantry. We found bread and peanut butter and made the best sandwich ever for a hungry, six year old boy. We ate this great meal while sitting on a large, stainless steel breadbox. My mother always used to laugh and say someday she was going to write a book about our trip and title it *Crossing the Pacific on a Breadbox*.

Once the typhoon passed, things settled down and life on the copra ship returned to normal. In the evenings, my mother would go and visit with the other passengers. She always thought that I was asleep, but soon after she left there would be a knock on our porthole. The Chief Engineer would lift me out and take me with him. I frequently sat in on his poker games and looked at his books. Before my mother returned to our stateroom he would slip me back through the porthole, so she did not know anything about my shenanigans. One afternoon she could not find me. After looking all around the ship she went to the bridge to ask for the Captain's help. The Captain was able to calm her by pointing out a small figure helping several crew members chipping paint on the forward deck. There I was happy as could be hard at work chipping paint even though the chipping bar was way too heavy for me to handle properly.

After a long, thirty days at sea we finally arrived at San Pedro Harbor in Los Angeles, California. The car was unloaded and once fueled it operated just fine, the smell of copra swirling around us as we drove away.

We waited for my father at my grandparent's house in Phoenix, Arizona. My father's departure from Manila was delayed because of an emergency hernia operation which became infected. The doctors would not release him in that condition. The delay went on for weeks and Mom was panicked. Fortunately, he had friends in the shipping industry and they began booking him on every available ship leaving Manila so that when he was ready, he would have a way out. The doctors finally conceded that with the threat of war, staying was too dangerous and they released him. He left on the last commercial ship out of Manila before the Japanese attack.

The Japanese bombed Manila on December 8, 1941, the same day that Pearl Harbor was attacked.[7] My parents worried about their many friends who remained in Manila, some of whom had elected to stay because of property and business. They had assumed that they would be confined to their houses for the remainder of the war; they were sadly mistaken. The Japanese treated foreign civilian prisoners harshly and there were many atrocities. Most of them were held in the infamous Santo Tomas and Los Banŏs internment camps under the cruelest conditions. After the liberation of the Philippines in 1945, I remember my parents poring over the lists of survivors of the Philippine occupation hoping in vain to find the names of their friends. My mother was in tears over the many friends that did not survive the war.

During college, my father had enlisted in Army ROTC and was commissioned as an Army Reserve Cavalry Second Lieutenant. In those days the U.S. Cavalry were horse mounted troops. By the time of World War II, the cavalry had become mechanized and his training in horsemanship would have been of little use in the current army. Because of his expertise in metallurgy, he was deferred from the draft and assigned as Director of War Materials at the National Academy of Sciences in Washington, D.C. We lived in Arlington, Virginia, and experienced the usual war shortages, gas rationing, ration cards, and food scarcity, but we were able to live in relative comfort.

After World War II my family moved to Columbus, Ohio, and dad took a management position at Battelle Memorial Institute. Battelle was a large nonprofit research company which did research in many areas of industry and for the U.S. government.

Our new home in Upper Arlington, a suburb of Columbus, was near the Scioto River and visiting and picnicking by the river became one of my summer pastimes. The river had two dams; the southern one nearest to our home made a long, narrow lake suitable for small power boats, canoes, and kayaks. Above the northern dam was a larger lake mostly used by sailboats. Like many eleven year old kids, I was interested in the small boats on the river and badgered my dad to help me build a fourteen foot runabout. He was a great teacher and while

---

[7] It was December 8, not December 7, because Manila was west of the International Date Line.

he would give advice and encouragement, I had to do all of the work. I built that first boat on the porch in the spring and launched it a couple of months later. I spent all of my paper route savings on a new, seven horsepower Mercury outboard motor and spent that summer happily running up and down the lower lake in all of my free time.

By the fall I had done everything I could do with that boat and was ready for a new experience. If I wanted to go faster, I would have to buy a larger motor; I was losing interest. One day my dad took me to the upper dam and we went sailing with a friend of his in a sailboat. This was an epiphany for me, for I realized that in sailing there were many new challenges and skills to learn. How well the boat sailed depended on the skill and experience of the skipper and the crew, not the size of a motor. Sailboat racing would be one of my ultimate challenges and great loves

**This photograph shows my first experience
sailing on that Interlake class sailboat**

During the winter my dad and I, with several of his Battelle friends, built a trimaran sailboat. It had a twenty-six foot main hull and two, sixteen foot pontoons. This boat was way before its time! We soon found that race committees at regattas could not classify the boat and assign it a handicap, therefore, we could not race. Ultimately we found a club that would accept us and began racing at the Leather Lips Yacht Club, named for an Indian chief from that area. That small yacht club on the Scioto River devised an unusual handicap system for the club trophy. After each race of the summer series the handicap for the next race adjusted the finish times so that if each boat sailed at the same speed as in the previous race they would finish at the same corrected time. This system seemed good at first because it would benefit those who were getting better, but the race committee did not account for the major changes in crew performance over the season and the various wind speeds. As it was, we were a very green crew and sailing a multihull boat was much more difficult than sailing a monohull. Each week we got better at handling the boat and the wind speed got progressively stronger as the season went on, which helped us more than others. The result was that the last race of the year was the only race that we were actually first to finish, but we finished first on "corrected time" for all the races and swept the series. The Yacht Club officers and the race committee hated the results and really did not like our multihull boat; it was not traditional enough. As far as I know they never used that particular handicap system again.

The following winter my dad and I built a Comet class sailboat in our dining room. As you might imagine my mother was in the running for sainthood for putting up with this arrangement. Sawdust and wood shavings were everywhere and covered everything. We used the dining room because our garage was not heated and we would have been unable to get a finished hull out of our below-grade basement. The next spring at the age of fourteen, I began racing my own boat in the "one design" Comet fleet. Having a fleet of eight to ten identical boats was challenging since your sailing ability meant everything. One of my competitors was very experienced and hard to beat, forcing me to study sailing and racing tactics.

Sailing was a transformational experience for me. I loved the wind whipping along, the spray of water off the bow, and the feel of the boat urging me to go faster in a high wind or to drift in lighter breezes.

Sailing gave me confidence and drew me closer to both my mom and dad since we spent so much time traveling to and sailing in various regattas. I had some success and became the local Comet Fleet Champion, which led to qualifying and racing in the Comet National Championship. One thing I learned from that experience was that there were a lot of really good sailors out there, many of whom had much better equipment than I had. Sailing was now in my blood.

=====

When I first expressed my interest in going to the Naval Academy, one of my high school classmates said, "You know Dave the U.S. Navy doesn't have any more ships with sails." He was wrong. Fairings covering submarine bridges and masts are commonly called sails.

Indeed the sails on the *Guardfish*, the submarine I would command twenty years later, extended over twenty-five feet above the hull of the submarine itself. Yet on the trail of K 184, this sail would not broach the surface, only the periscope and communications masts would ever be exposed. Submarine warfare carried out with stealth was most closely likened to the covert actions of great spies: get in, get close, listen silently, and most of all, don't get caught.

CHAPTER III

Becoming a Qualified Submarine Officer

ДОРОГА К МОРЮ *(Road to the Sea)*

Twelve year old Alfred Berzin

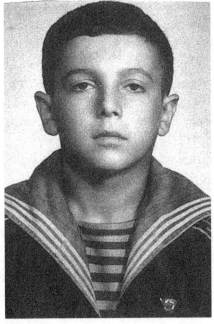

In 1945, at the age of twelve, future Rear Admiral Alfred Berzin became a pupil at the Riga Nakhimov Naval Academy in Latvia. Six years later, in June 1951, he graduated, having completed his basic naval training. After the graduation ceremony, Berzin and his fellow cadets were granted liberty then went to Leningrad to continue with advanced studies in the First Baltic Naval Academy. In the morning of July 15, 1951, the train arrived at Warsaw Station, and the new students walked to the school. There, they were handed over for education purposes to Lieutenant Gruzdev, nicknamed Peter. The lieutenant was a graduate of the College of Coastal Defense and a monster both inside and out. He was paranoid about keeping the latrine in immaculate condition. Everyone received a full course of instruction in this regard. When it came time for sentry duty at the latrine, Peter would examine each cadet with his shifty eyes and say with his slight lisp, "Do not let the cadets drink water from the urinals. Make sure that each cadet uses no more than four pieces of toilet paper, and then throw them into the basket. Make sure that papers with portraits of the Party leaders are not thrown into the toilet as well…" and so on. He also had a speech about badges. He said the students should wear their Komsomol badges on the left side of one's flannel shirt at the level of our nipple yet two fingers to the right.[8] More important badges go two fingers down. It was a very regimented life.

From day one, it became clear which subjects would be of great use in the future. There was extensive reading and writing, advanced physics, advanced mathematics, analytical geometry, astronomy, navigation, and naval history. Berzin's favorite subject, astronomy, was taught by Captain Second Rank Vereshchagin, who was quite an expert in his field. The daily routine was so busy that there was little leisure time. Four hours of class in the morning, a one hour lunch break, two more hours of training, dinner, two hours of mandatory homework, a walk before bed check-in, and then lights out.

There were three companies of first year cadets and each company lived in a big room separated from the other companies by a small passage. Each room had a nightstand (the nightstand was a small table with a cabinet that served as a guard station) where the cadets on watch were stationed. The cadets on watch were not allowed to sleep

---

[8] Komsomol badges signified that the wearer was a member of the Young Communist League.

at night, so they slept in the first half of the day. On a typical day, six people were up every night. Whose idea was it? Who knows? But it was as if they expected some Martian invasion, although the cadets on guard had nothing but an armband to resist the attackers.

One night, when it was Berzin's turn to be on duty, he wandered off the post to sit on his bed. At that very moment Army Colonel Sokolov, the Duty Officer, doing his night rounds, showed up. He immediately noticed the infringement and angrily uttered, "Ten days arrest."

Berzin was marched off to the guardhouse. For the next ten days, he and his fellow cellmates were shipped to the trolley park, where they carried bricks on stretchers. By the evening, their hands were blistered with blood. Their berths or 'planes', as they were called, consisted of a frame of wooden rails; the students used their pea coats as blankets. The berths were fastened to the walls of the cell in such a manner that one could only sit on the floor, which was not allowed. The guards hovered closely, watching through the peephole in the door. The lights never went out.

It would be Berzin's first and only trip to the guardhouse. Once was enough. By the end of May 1952, having passed his first year exam, he and his fellow cadets left for training with the Northern Fleet.

They arrived at the Northern Fleet with a depot ship (floating base) and torpedo boats that came to the Soviet Union during WWII. They were lend-lease from England and the U.S.: *Vospers* and *Higgins* boats as well as *Luhrs*, which were trophies from Germany. Under the leadership of Captain Second Rank Vereshchagin, the cadets studied astronomy, measuring the heights of the stars and solving problems in determining locations.

Most of the time was spent training on the floating base, which would sometimes go to sea, giving the students the chance to practice plotting (navigation). They slept in the crew's quarters and did their homework in the petty officers' cabin. The Political Officer had papered the walls with political slogans, such as, "The Army and the Navy are the Homeland's Stronghold," "From dawn to dawn, sailors are on watch," "Know the sea by the wave," "The rudder cannot be put overboard," "The Soviet lighthouse is seen from afar," "A soldier beats the enemy in the field and a sailor at sea."

Long Bay was surrounded by hills that could have snow on them even in the middle of June. There was no vegetation, only callous moss. The sun never went down; it was light both day and night in the summer.

In his second year at the Academy, Berzin's superiors informed his class that they would be switching to a submarine curriculum. On submarines in those days, cadets trained with artillery, studying their structure and operational use. There was a simulator where cadets, guided only by the sound of falling shells conducted artillery fire. Aiming the artillery or "fire control" was directed by a stereoscopic telescope with a corrugated flexible hose and megaphone through which the orders were given.

In August 1954, Berzin was third year student at the Naval Academy when he and his schoolmates boarded a train of freight cars equipped and filled with double stacked bunks on either side of the door. They slept in their clothes on plain wooden boards again using their pea coats as blankets and duffel bags, filled with simple possessions, as pillows. The train started out for Arkhangelsk (Archangel), a western port in the far north of Russia, at the delta where the Dvina River meets the White Sea. Founded more than a thousand years ago, Arkhangelsk is said to be protected by the Archangel Michael. It is home to a thriving maritime community.

There the students were provided bread, sugar, and canned meat called "horse," since no one knew exactly what it was. At the station stops, all would grab their kettles and run to the booths that had a sign saying "hot water," fill them up, and dash back to the train cars. The food rations were monotonous. Many smoked cheap tobacco, so the car became filled with thick, swirling smoke. In the aisle, there were boxes of precision instruments: sextants, chronometers, deck watches, and star globes. Taking advantage of the fact that the superiors were traveling in a staff car elsewhere along the train, the cadets used the tops of these boxes to play cards. On the upper bunk, someone could be heard playing the guitar and singing in a gravelly voice about "some teeth chattering on the piano keys" in the way a prison song is sung.

Through the open doorway of the freight car there were glimpses of the forest and lonely houses looking old and sad. Not far from Arkhangelsk the train came to a stop. There was mud everywhere and walkways of rotten, rough cut wood stretched between crooked little houses. The journey continued apace. Finally the train arrived in Arkhangelsk. Warehouses, factories, and ships were all that one could see. The Dvina River was wide and powerful there. When the train arrived at the naval training vessel, *Neman*, everyone began to fuss and run around. The duffel bags were carried up and down the ladders; everybody was shouting, grabbing mattresses, and scrambling for a bunk. Warrant Officer Spitsyn chased after the cadets because the boxes with precision instruments had to be loaded carefully on board. Everyone was shouting and agreeing with the warrant officer that the boxes indeed had to be carried on board, however, nobody did anything about it and instead kept looking for their caps and duffel bags. Eventually everything settled down everyone got situated, and the cruise began.

A tugboat towed the ship away from the pier, out into the waterway and, after being released, the *Neman* headed out on a course with what seemed like an infinite number of alignments (course corrections and navigation changes), the maneuvers announced loudly by someone with a nasal voice. The route was from Arkhangelsk to Novaya Zemlya, where the ship was to transport a company of construction engineers (similar to the U.S. Navy Seabees).

The company commander, Captain Sidorov, sat in the stern of the ship with a dog named Nadya. The Captain was bored and Nadya probably was too. A small sailboat loaded with hay passed on the starboard side. It had a black pirate sail and a big woman dressed in a quilted jacket rowing away. Instructed to plot the *Neman's* course on the open deck where tables were covered with maps, forms, and navigation logs, the cadets were divided into three working shifts; each shift was eight hours long. In the beginning, everyone was excited and worked hard taking the maximum number of bearings, running from tables to the rangefinder, busy like bees, and encouraging each other with jokes.

As each hour passed, however, the weather got worse, the wind got stronger, and the waves grew higher. Somewhere in the middle of the way to Novaya Zemlya, the *Neman* began pitching and rolling quite a lot. Several of the cadets soon fell on their bunks and lay flat, slightly moaning (seasick). However, most of them toughened up and went on working. To stave off hunger, the men kept on plotting and eating "rusks" (pieces of stale bread, usually eaten with tea and herring. The herring appeared rusty because they were pickled in cans and some of the metal transfers to the fish giving it a rusty look and taste).

The construction engineers traveling to Novaya Zemlya looked baby-faced and innocent; each one smoked cheap tobacco. They were having fun sitting in the stern and spitting carelessly into the raging sea. Nadya, the lonely dog, ran around the ship. Her eyes were sad; she felt seasick and could only eat sugar. It was four in the morning when Berzin got off duty and was sent to the crew quarters in the forecastle to get some sleep. The sound of the water splashing through the scuppers on the deck swept rhythmically in unison with the rolling of the ship. Next to the ladder, a huge bucket containing the contents of many stomachs slid back and forth, "evil spirits" (foul odors) floated between the bunks. In the darkness, someone snored like a rhino. Those stricken with seasickness gathered amidships where there was less pitching and rolling. Everyone had their pockets full of rusks, a rusty herring in their hands, and cheeks that were deathly pale. It was cold.

Finally the *Neman* arrived at Novaya Zemlya and dropped anchor. The coastline was made up of flat stones and low banks. The sun came out but it didn't get any warmer. Water, stone, and clouds made the view icy cold. From there, the ship sailed to Murmansk to the Norwegian Sea to Kaliningrad.

The following year, 1955, Berzin and his classmates traveled to Sebastopol in freight cars for almost a week, crossing the country from north to south. Upon arrival, they were divided into groups and each group was assigned to a different submarine. Berzin's group was assigned to the submarine commanded by Captain Second Rank Semyonov and his subordinate, Navigator – Lieutenant Lazarev.

Back at the Academy, the cadets had learned the ins and outs of a submarine. Within a week on board, all were confident they could perform such tasks sealing a leak and pressuring or draining any compartment. They learned how to use electronic navigation devices, as well as repair them and find failures with the equipment. They studied submarine tactics, the theory and practice of torpedo firing, and continued to perfect our navigational skills. The last year of school flew by. The time had come for the State Examinations and Submarine Navigations tests.

Finally, on September 3, 1955, Alfred Berzin's class at the Baltic Naval Academy graduated. Each student was given an invitation card with the picture of a submarine and a naval flag on it. The invitation opened with an epigraph:

> *"Comrades, you have graduated from the Academy where you got your first lessons of toughness. But the school is only a preparatory stage. The true toughening experience will come outside of school, overcoming difficulties in your everyday life."*

> *J.V. Stalin*

The head of the Academy, Rear Admiral Egipko, awarded each graduate his golden lieutenant shoulder straps and a dagger, wishing them a happy voyage and "to surface as many times as [you] submerge." Each one was ready to start his own voyage. All were full of hope. It was a system of training not unlike that which was had by Rear Admiral Berzin's future counterpart in the United States of America.

BECOMING A QUALIFIED U.S. SUBMARINE OFFICER

While I was in high school, I prepared for college entrance exams and discussed college and career choices with my parents. The U.S. Naval Academy at Annapolis was considered, but I thought it might be something best pursued after one or two years of college. I was only seventeen and I knew that many of the candidates were much older than me and would have had some college experience. Since my dad was a mining engineer and metallurgist, I was also very interested in following in his footsteps. He recommended the University of Cornell because they had an excellent metallurgy department and he knew and respected some of the professors in that department.

I applied to the University of Cornell and visited the campus. Typical of my age, I was most impressed by a young girl there and with the fraternity parties. I applied for a Naval Reserve Officers Training Corps (NROTC) scholarship and was accepted, but there was no space in the NROTC unit at Cornell. As an alternative, my dad recommended the University of Missouri, but I could not see myself going to Missouri. When I finally thought I might have to go to school locally at Ohio State University in Columbus, Ohio, my dad came to my rescue. He had heard that the United States Naval Academy entrance exam was being given at the main post office in downtown Columbus. So off I went to take the exam. It wasn't much different from the other college entrance exams I had recently taken and I passed. Now I needed to find a U.S. Senator or Congressman with an appointment still available. Ohio Congressman John M. Vorys had a third alternate vacancy and this allowed me to go through the interviews and physical exam process held at Naval Station Great Lakes. Again I passed and to my surprise the principal appointee decided not to accept the appointment and one of the other alternates was unable to pass the physical. Now I was a first alternate, which is sort of like being a bridesmaid. My dad found out through his friends that Ohio Senator John W. Bricker had another first alternate appointment available. Dad called me one morning, told me to put on my best suit and to be at the Senator's office at 10 o'clock. That was an unnerving experience since I did not have the luxury of preparing myself for this interview. When I got to the Senator's office, I waited in his outer room for a short time and then was escorted into his private office. He had me sit down and asked me several questions about myself and why I wanted to go to the Naval Academy. I must have done pretty well because after asking me for a second time if I really wanted to go to the academy and my immediate affirmation, he swiveled around in his chair, picked up a white phone which was his direct line to his Washington, D.C. office, and told his assistant to put my name on the appointment. He then stood up and shook my hand. I thanked him for the appointment and left his office. It was all over in such a short time my head was swimming. I was lucky, both primary appointees declined their appointments and I got in.

My U.S. Naval Academy class of 1956 started with 1057 students and finally graduated with only 681. Attrition was due to academic failures, resignations, bad conduct discharges, and physical disqualifications; this represented a loss of thirty-six percent of my class. Getting through the academy was no piece of cake. While the studying and regimentation were grueling, the opportunity to sail both for recreation and on the Navy's intercollegiate-sailing team was my salvation. During my plebe summer, when I first arrived at the Academy, I was able to take a sailing weekend on one of the Academy yawls, a twenty-five foot sailboat. The boat was skippered by a junior staff officer and crewed by me and five classmates and we enjoyed sailing across the Chesapeake Bay to a small protected inlet for the night. As we approached the inlet, one of the black, rain squalls that the Chesapeake is well known for, dumped on us. The skipper and I were the only experienced sailors on board and we remained topside to take the boat into the inlet and anchor in the driving rainstorm. We were both very cold and wet, but when we went below decks were greeted by a well prepared dinner and the warmth of the cabin. One of my classmates on board had been a ship's cook before coming to the Naval Academy. I can't remember any meal as welcome as that one. Returning to the Naval Academy the next day as the sun was setting, I watched a family sailing on a fair sized, cruising sailboat; husband and wife were at the wheel and two young kids were playing in the netting below the bowsprit. This sight made me set a goal, which I finally achieved many many years later when I bought and finished a Westsail 32 (shown below at Eagle Point in the Washington State San Juan Islands). After retiring from the Navy in 1980, my wife, Marilyn, and our teenage daughter, Daveylyn, sailed and lived on this boat for a year and a half until we settled in Southern California.

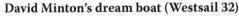

David Minton's dream boat (Westsail 32)

Once the academic year began, I went out for the intercollegiate sailing team. At that time, the only college team racing was done in dinghies, small cat rigged sailboats. Teams entered one boat in each of two divisions, A and B, and their combined scores determined the regatta winner. The boats we used at the Naval Academy were Tempest dinghies, a two-person catboat.

The following picture shows me and my crew for the first three years, Midshipman Richard (Dick) Roberts. During my fourth year, my crew was Otto Rice who, although inexperienced in sailboat racing, learned quickly and became an excellent crew.

I sailed on the dinghy team all four years, making the varsity team in my second year. During my third and fourth years we, the Navy team, were very successful, culminating in second place during the 1955 National Championships and first place in the 1956 National Championships. For the first time in the U.S. Naval Academy's history, we were the National Champions.

The 1956 Intercollegiate National Championship was sailed at the Crescent Sail Yacht Club on Lake St. Clair, Grosse Pointe, Michigan.

I was the captain of the team and sailed the Division A boat with my crew, Otto Rice, but the real heroes of the regatta were our Division B skipper, Jim Googe and his crew, Al Friedland. On the thirty-second race, the last race of the regatta, Brown University's skipper had a big enough lead in accumulative points to win the championship by simply finishing the race, even if he came in last. To win the championship, Navy would have to win the final race while Brown would have to foul out and not finish. Jim strategically positioned his boat to leeward of the Brown boat and forced it toward the windward end of the starting line, trapping it with no room left to maneuver when the starting gun went off. The Brown University skipper misjudged his position and their boat fouled the committee boat's anchor chain and was disqualified from the final race. All Jim had to do now was to beat the remaining fourteen boats to the finish. Having finished my last race, I watched from the roof of the yacht club. It was amazing. Jim had made a very good start and rounded the windward mark in second place. On the downwind leg he overtook the boat ahead of him and held his lead to the finish. To say there was pandemonium in the Navy team and its followers would be an understatement. That fall and spring, Navy had won all but one of the regattas on the East Coast. It was an unprecedented racing season.

At the end of my fourth year at the Academy, it came time to select our first duty station. The process was very simple. All of those who were going to Navy ship and aviator billets drew numbers and based on those numbers they could select a ship from the list of available billets. Almost all line officers wanted to go to destroyers because on a destroyer a young officer is exposed to lots of assignments and duties. The number I drew was not high enough for me to select a destroyer; there would be no destroyer billets left when it was my turn select. I began to look around at other ships and their scheduled operations and found an auxiliary-cargo ship, the USS *Arneb* (AKA 56) which was going to operate from Australia to Operation Deep Freeze in the Antarctic and I planned to select that ship. When it came time for me to select my assignment, four additional destroyers had just been added to the list, so I changed my mind and picked the USS *Bausell* (DD 845) out of San Diego. Some of my classmates, who drew better numbers than I, felt that they had been cheated by not having the opportunity to select those destroyers. And so it goes. Later while in Australia I met the classmate who had selected the *Arneb* and although he had some marvelous experiences both in the Antarctic and in Australia, I don't believe it was as good a professional choice as I was lucky enough to make.

After sailing in the Intercollegiate National Dinghy Championship, I reported to my first duty station, the *Bausell*, in San Diego. The ship was skippered by Commander Freiden, a post war Temporary Reserve Officer. I believe he was the only Temporary Reserve Officer with a destroyer command in the Pacific Fleet. Because of his unusual assignment he was very cautious and careful in his actions and in the operation of the ship. The *Bausell* was the flagship of the division with the Division Commander, Captain Sellers embarked. I was initially assigned as the electronics material officer, but quickly moved up to be the officer in charge of the Combat Information Center (CIC) and doubled as Captain Sellers's CIC Officer. I was soon qualified as an Officer of the Deck. These additional responsibilities were very rewarding and exciting.

As a green Ensign I clearly remember our first gunnery firing exercise. I was assigned as the check-fire observer in the number one gun mount. The exercise we were conducting was to fire at a target sleeve being towed by a small airplane and my job was to make sure that the fire control system was tracking the sleeve, not the aircraft. On the very first firing run the Gunnery Officer ordered, "Commence firing" and because my sights were on the airplane, I ordered, "Check-Fire" and released the automatic switch which prevented the guns from firing. All hell broke out! The Gunnery Officer came down from the bridge and screamed at me, using some swear words that even I had never heard. After he calmed down and let me explain what I had seen, he realized that I had done the right thing and may have prevented a serious incident. I never was completely sure that this whole event wasn't staged as a test of the new Ensign. It taught me an important lesson: you should always be alert and ready to take action.

The skipper soon assigned me as the Maneuvering Watch Officer of the Deck giving me the opportunity to improve my ship handling skills.

In 1957, we had a wonderful visit in Melbourne, Australia. Our division of four destroyers and an auxiliary oiler were the first U.S. Navy ships to visit Melbourne since World War II. The city went out of its way to entertain us. On our first day in port we were invited to three cocktail parties. The first was hosted by the City of Melbourne. The second was by the Australian Navy and was very interesting because we were able to meet our counterparts. I was surprised that they were a lot older than me. Many of their officers were stuck at their rank and position, leaving little chance to advance; I really felt bad about their predicament. The third party was in the basement of the Madera Wine Company with music for dancing. The host had invited many young Melbourne models. Of course this party was one of the highlights of our visit.

During World War II Australians felt that the United States Navy had saved them from the Japanese, so many went out of their way to greet and thank us during that trip. One day I was walking on a downtown street and was stopped by an elderly man who had served in North Africa. He grabbed me by the arm and would not let me go until I agreed to let him buy me a drink. Because Australia had lost a large number of their men, the young ladies were anxious to meet our officers and enlisted men. While we were in port, the city was also having a celebration called the "Moomba Festival." Moomba is an aborigine word which means, "Let's get together" and I believe it was taken quite literally.

After we left port, the *Bausell* transited independently across the Coral Sea from Melbourne to Manus Island, Papua New Guinea.[9] The Coral Sea has many small, low lying islands and hundreds of reefs, many of which were still uncharted. Late in the afternoon, sonar reported a submerged coral head off our port bow. As Officer of the Deck I slowed the ship and called the Captain. We proceeded gradually as

---

[9] In the beginning of World War II Manus Island was the site of an observation post manned by the Australian Navy, who also provided medical treatment to the inhabitants. Manus was first bombed by the Japanese on January 25, 1942 and several hundred Japanese soldiers swarmed ashore. With limited resources, the Australians withdrew to the jungle. Later in 1942, Japan established a military base on Manus. This was attacked and reclaimed by U.S. forces in February 1944. An allied naval base was established on the island and it later supported the British Pacific Fleet.

sonar continued to report more and more coral heads. Most of these were on our port side which led us to alter course to starboard to give more space between us and the huge colonies of coral. The Operations Officer joined the sonarmen and the Captain and I remained on the bridge. Hours passed and the situation continued to get worse.

As the sun was beginning to set, sonar reported that there was a solid reef wall in front of us, but there seemed to be a "soft spot" off to our right which could be deep enough for us to pass through the reef. The Captain had our gig lowered and sent it ahead to take soundings of this "soft spot." Because of the seriousness of the situation, the Captain graciously took the conn (directional control of the ship), so I wouldn't be involved if we ran aground. The soundings indicated that there was adequate depth for us to pass. We moved ahead slowly and when we crossed what we thought was the reef, we found ourselves in a little bay nearly surrounded by coral. Again sonar reported that there was a "soft spot" ahead and when the gig went to investigate, they ran aground. The Captain wisely decided to anchor and wait for morning. After sunrise our predicament was obvious; we could see the underwater reef about three quarters of the way around us. Throughout the next day we wound ourselves back along the track we had entered until we came to deep water. It was interesting to note that later an old chart not in use reported a sighting of breakers in the area of our anchorage in the early 1800s. We filed a detailed report of our soundings and location, but I was unsuccessful in convincing the Navigator that we should name the location "Minton's Anchorage."

During our first Western Pacific deployment, I maneuvered the ship into and out of many foreign ports and even made some of the landings. It was an invaluable experience for a young, naval officer. I really liked the ship, the officers I worked with, and most of the crew. Since my division was part of the Operations Department, the sailors that worked for me were generally smarter and better trained than the crew as a whole. There was a group of exceptional, well educated, sailors that hung out together. The group consisted of a fire control man, a radioman, a yeoman, an electronics technician, and a sonarman. As a collateral duty I was also the Ship's Secretary which meant I oversaw the functions of the yeoman. One night after the ship's office was closed while I was reviewing some papers, I noticed a book about heraldry lying on the lead yeoman's desk. There was a paper marking one page of the book which showed a shield with a lion holding a beer mug and a phrase in Gaelic and English. The phrase was translated as "Mother, watch your daughter!" I thought nothing about it until we reached Yokosuka, Japan. One morning my best radar man, Reilly, had a patch sewn on his work jacket with this same shield, but no translation. As I was inspecting the division I stopped and looked closely at the patch and said, "That's Gaelic for 'mother, watch your daughter, isn't it?'" Reilly was shocked; he thought I could read Gaelic and I never told him otherwise. Later the group honored me with a coffee cup displaying the same shield. Now sixty years later I still use that cup. I hope mothers are still looking out for their daughters.

Once we returned from that deployment it was time for our skipper to be relieved and a new skipper to come aboard. Commander Turner was very different from Commander Friedan; he was relaxed and confident in his ability to handle the ship and the crew. The day after he joined us, we left San Diego Harbor and went out to a naval operating area just off the coast. The new skipper wanted to see how the ship and crew performed since his previous command had been a small oiler. We ran at flank speed, backed emergency, held man-overboard drills, and all sorts of other maneuvers and drills. As usual I had the deck and when the skipper was satisfied he said to me, "Dave, take her to the barn!" and he went to his sea cabin.

I looked around realizing I was really in charge. I turned the ship for the channel entrance. Once in the channel, I reported our position to the Captain using the voice tube that connected his sea cabin to the bridge. And so it went, I made reports as we took various courses following the channel and he would reply, "Very well." Once inside the inner harbor, we passed through the seaplane landing area which always gave us some concern because seaplanes have the right of way, but never told us when they were coming. Still with no captain on the bridge, I turned to make the final approach for a starboard side landing alongside the tender. The Captain finally appeared and said to me, "I'm sorry Dave, but I want to make my first landing on *Bausell*," and with that he took the conn. While I was aboard he never made another landing and let me and the other junior officers get as much experience as possible. He was a great example of what a leader should be.

Before our second deployment to the Western Pacific, several experienced officers were transferred and we were shorthanded for qualified Officers of the Deck. Part of the trip across the Pacific Ocean we operated independently instead of in concert with other ships, so the skipper used this time to train the new Ensigns. Never have I seen a group that had less knowledge and common sense. There was one instance when a temporarily qualified Officer of the Deck just left the bridge unsupervised to go to the head two decks below. The Captain happened to leave his sea cabin and found the bridge unmanned, which is a serious breach of protocol. That was what he had to deal with.

When we joined the rest of the division and the carrier, only two of us were qualified to take the watch during plane guard duty. The plane guard station for our destroyer was close to the port bow of the carrier in a position to rescue the pilot if a plane went into the drink. Because the carrier had to frequently change course, often without warning, to keep the wind right on her bow when planes were taking off, the Officer of the Deck on our ship had to be constantly vigilant and never take his eyes off the carrier. With only two qualified officers, it made for some long watches. When the *Bausell* was positioned in front of the carrier as part of the screen protecting the carrier from other ships or submarines we had three qualified Officers of the Deck. Because of all of the regular day duties for the Officer of the Deck, three officers is not enough, but to make it even more complicated, the task force conducted night Combat Information Center (CIC) drills requiring me to be present at that time also. I was getting almost no sleep, so I had a bunk mattress brought up to CIC and when I could, I slept under one of the plotting displays. One day while I was Officer of the Deck and struggling to stay awake, the skipper took pity on me, relieved me of the watch, and sent me below for some much needed sleep.

As a young officer I had not fully decided on a career path, but for some time I had been considering submarine duty. Because my wife's uncle, Rear Admiral Larry Julihn, USN (Ret.), was such an inspiring man and a submarine hero of World War II, I decided to apply for submarine school. While the *Bausell* was still working with the carrier, I was invited over to the carrier by several of the pilots I had worked with as the *Bausell's* air controller. The skipper agreed with this arrangement and as I was getting ready to high line to the carrier, which is sort of like zip lining, the yeoman gave me a letter that had just come in. The letter contained my orders to submarine school in Groton, Connecticut later that year. Once aboard the carrier I found my pilot friends and knowing pilots always had a little illegal booze on board, I was able to celebrate my new orders with a drink or two.

Bausell's next assignment was off the coast of Singapore in the event American citizens needed to be evacuated due to unrest in the area. We had been at sea for some time, the weather was hot and humid, and the living spaces on this class of destroyer had no air conditioning. For days we steamed around at slow speed on a glassy sea, the only thing moving were poisonous sea snakes swimming on the surface. The crew had almost reached its limit and there had been several fights. One afternoon after working hours, the skipper had the gunners mate bring his forty-five caliber pistol to the bridge. He then did an amazing feat. While sitting on his bridge chair, he calmly fired round after round at the snakes cutting them into pieces. Almost all of the crew was on deck and took this all in. They knew he was "the Man."

Our trip off of Singapore was unnecessary and we were finally sent to Subic Bay, Philippines for liberty. This was one of the most depraved ports in the world and the crew loved it, but the base commander wisely limited liberty in Olongapo to midnight. This was frequently referred to as "Cinderella liberty." San Miguel was the beer of choice and the object seemed to drink as much as you can before midnight. The first night in port I was the In Port Officer of the Deck, which meant I had to stay aboard and check everyone in when they returned. As the mostly drunk sailors returned to the ship, I would stop each one individually and take away any alcohol they were carrying or had strapped to their legs and drop it overboard. This was a tough job and many of the crew were not happy. After midnight things began to quiet down, but the conditions in the living quarters were untenable without air conditioning and all those who could walk, congregated on deck either on the forecastle or the fantail. The results were fights started up first on the fantail and then on the forecastle. I had two petty officers with me armed with billy clubs. We broke up one fight after another. Even more dangerous than the fights was several of the crew deciding to go for a swim off the fantail; not only were they very drunk, but the water was extremely polluted. After some time I was able to coach all of the swimmers back on board, at least I hoped that we hadn't lost one. We wouldn't know for sure until tomorrow at muster. Fortunately all were accounted for the next morning.

During the last part of the watch, things had quieted down again and I was looking forward to the sun rising and being relieved of the watch. I was standing on the deck with my back to the passageway when a sailor from the engineering department stole quietly up behind me from the inboard passageway. He had armed himself with a meat cleaver from the galley and in his drunken condition, had set out to kill the Officer of the Deck — me. I was completely unaware of his approach, but much to my good fortune, the petty officer on watch with me was behind me in the dark passageway. He saw the sailor raise the meat cleaver above my head and grabbed him from behind in a full nelson hold. He and I then wrestled the weapon away from my assailant and locked him in a nearby line locker until he could be transferred to the brig. This all happened so fast I did not have time to be frightened. Later the seriousness of the attack came home. I owed my life to my shipmate, Tiny, who was always called by that nickname because he was anything but tiny. After that experience I was really looking forward to my transfer to submarine school; it couldn't come too soon.

Like my previous duty stations, Submarine School had its challenges, but I was happy with the studies and short indoctrination cruises. After sub school in January 1958, I was ordered to the USS *Gudgeon* (SS 567), a diesel boat whose home port was Pearl Harbor, Hawaii. My experience as Officer of the Deck on *Bausell* and as a small boat skipper led to my almost immediate qualification as a Surface Officer of the Deck on *Gudgeon*. I was first assigned as the Junior Officer of the Deck to move the boat from the Pearl Harbor pier to the West Lock weapons pier to load torpedoes. The skipper had me get the boat underway, maneuver through the West Lock channel, and make the landing at the weapons pier. I also made the transit back to our original Pearl Harbor pier and luckily made a perfect "one bell landing" (only having to back down once). The skipper then shook my hand and stated that I was qualified as the Officer of the Deck. That was a blast!

Submarine School graduates were trained and nearly ready to qualify as a Diving Officer of the watch on their first assignment. On our first day at sea I was given the Diving Officer watch and the Senior Watch Officer assigned the Chief of the Boat, a qualified Diving Officer, to keep an eye on me. During that watch a young, interior communication (IC) electrician came to me and asked me to teach him how to use the log scales on his slide rule. What a change from my days on the *Bausell*!

Ever since that day I have described that experience as one of two bookends. The first bookend was the attempt on my life that night in Subic Bay and the second was the request for my help with slide rule log scales by a young petty officer. There was now no question that I had made the right decision to volunteer for submarine duty. The all-volunteer officers and crew on submarines were intelligent and professional, I felt comfortable in my new environment, and it was like I had finally come home. I stayed in the submarine force for the remainder of my twenty-four years in active service.

During my tour on *Gudgeon* we made one six month Western Pacific (WestPac) deployment which included a sixty day special operation. The next year, instead of going back to WestPac we were assigned a cruise to the Puget Sound Washington area. We called it an EastPac deployment.

The *Gudgeon* was assigned two major operations during this deployment. The first EastPac operation was to conduct a month long test of Mark 45 and Mark 37-1 torpedoes in Dabob Bay. This deep water bay was outfitted with a three dimensional acoustical range which could accurately track the performance of instrumented weapons. As Weapons Officer I began most days at five o'clock, in the rain loading torpedoes for that day's testing. We got underway at 7 o'clock for the short run from the Bangor Weapons Station to Dabob Bay and returned to the Weapons Station before nightfall. On one occasion the Commanding Officer decided, just for fun, to make a submerged approach to the pier. The water in Hood Canal is very deep, making a submerged approach feasible, but we did not take into account the ebb current pushing us away from the pier, nor the fact that once we surfaced our mooring lines, which were stowed in lockers topside, were not immediately available. The Commanding Officer made the submerged approach and surfaced the boat. I rushed to the bridge to take the conn but was helpless to complete the landing because the deck crew was unable to get the lines up before we drifted away from the pier. The line handlers on the pier could not believe what they had just seen and were rolling with laughter at our predicament. Once the deck crew was ready, I went ahead and made a much more standard landing. There was a lesson there somewhere.

The second EastPac operation's objective was to test an experimental sound reducing snorkel exhaust mast installed at the Puget Sound Naval Shipyard. Diesel noise transmitted through the water while snorkeling (submerged with periscope and air intake above the surface) made diesel boats easy to detect. A test mast was erected on the after-deck containing an interior sound damping bladder which could be inflated or deflated with air to optimize the mast's sound reduction properties. Because of heat buildup and the mast's inherent strength, this test mast could only be used with the submarine submerged and stationary.

During the testing of the experimental mast, I had my first experience with submerging a submarine while being suspended from mooring buoys. As the Diving Officer I was responding to the Commanding Officer's orders. I had compensated the *Gudgeon* to be very light and then by cycling the main ballast tank vent valves we slowly submerged as the ballast tanks filled with seawater. The Captain watched through the periscope the displacement marks on the mooring buoys. These marks indicated the amount of load the submarine was placing on the two buoys. As necessary, he ordered seawater flooded into our internal variable ballast tanks. Slowly we achieved a condition of being slightly heavy and balanced the strain on both the forward and after mooring buoys. Thus we were submerged suspended evenly on chains equipped with emergency disconnects from both mooring buoys. Topside the divers were in the water beginning to install hydrophones along the pressure hull to measure our radiated noise. At this point the Captain, Commander Scoggins, said, "I guess we are submerged" and he personally sounded the ship's diving alarm. This action had an unanticipated consequence!

Standing orders for the Maneuvering Room Watch required the watch to go ahead standard on both screws when the diving alarm was sounded. No one had told maneuvering to ignore those orders on this occasion. When the electrician brought the motors to the ahead standard position, the submarine jumped ahead, breaking the emergency disconnects from both mooring buoys, and making the divers scramble to get clear. Fortunately no one was hurt. The Captain had only himself to blame. A considerable time passed before the disconnect links could be replaced and the sound trials could continue.

After returning to the shipyard the Engineer Officer took a month's leave while assigning Lieutenant Junior Grade Richard C. Camacho (Dick) and me to supervise the replacement and testing of a new generator. This was a major repair project entailing cutting a large hole in the hull and many of the *Gudgeon's* piping systems, which were in the way. The shipyard was courting the submarine force for a share of the lucrative submarine work and was eager to make a good impression. It turned out to be a good experience for both Dick and me, but we probably drove the shipyard crazy with our demands and perhaps overly conservative testing requirements.

I volunteered for the nuclear training program in 1961 and was sent back to Washington, D.C. to be interviewed by Admiral Rickover and his staff. Because of my father's earlier interaction with Rickover, I had a unique interview experience with the Admiral. My father, David C. Minton, Jr., was director of Battelle Memorial Institute in Columbus, Ohio. At the same time I was at the United States Naval Academy in Annapolis, Rickover (then a Captain) contracted Battelle to develop a process to refine Zirconium for fuel element cladding. Rickover visited the Columbus labs many times and became a nuisance to the scientists working on the Zirconium Project.[10] My father, the director, threw him out of his office several times for interfering with the scientists' work. About this time my father realized that I might want to enter the submarine service and that he might have made this career move difficult for me, so he assigned another senior manager at Battelle to deal directly with Rickover. My father's concern was justified because, of course, we have the same name. There would be no mistaken identification.

In my first interview for the nuclear power program, Admiral Rickover threw me out of his office four separate times. The first time was before I had said anything. The system for conducting these interviews used two prospective, commanding officers-in-training at the Naval Reactors Office. One sat in the Admiral's office to take notes of the interview. He was referred to as the "inside man." The "outside man" was there to literally catch and council the interviewee when he came out of the office. If the interviewee was going to see Rickover again, he would be escorted to a desk in an empty office to think about what he had said and what he should have said. Being thrown out of Rickover's office one time was not unusual. The second time was cause for concern. The third time caused a great deal of excitement. While I was in his office the fourth time, the Admiral described my weaknesses and shortcomings in great detail ending with "...even your father should be ashamed of you."

Despite this less than encouraging interview, I was accepted into the program. In retrospect, I believe the Admiral was just having fun

---

[10] Admiral Rickover, then Captain Rickover, and his staff were convinced that pure Zirconium was the superior option for reactor fuel element cladding. The problem was that there was no process to refine the Zirconium in quantities need by the submarine program. After a while being irritated by Captain Rickover's frequent visits and interference with his research, the Battelle Memorial Institute chief metallurgist, Ervin Eastman, decided to abandon the quest for a suitable process to refine the Zirconium and without authority began working on alloying the Zirconium with other elements. This process ultimately led to an alloy called Zircaloy which was much easier to refine in the required quantities. Eastman was quoted as saying "I have never seen a pure metal that couldn't be made better as an alloy." Zircaloy is now the standard for all U.S. naval reactors.

at my expense and getting back at my father through me. As a young officer, I was in shock. Later I learned that he possessed a great sense of humor.

I was accepted into the nuclear power program, but the next training class was full. So the Admiral put me into a forty hour per week study program. I was given a stack of books to study while continuing my duties on board USS *Gudgeon* (SS 567). I worked hard to meet both requirements. Six months later I was ordered back to Washington, D.C. to be tested and to be interviewed again by Admiral Rickover. I had religiously recorded the hours I used on shipboard duties and the hours that I had studied. The total hours worked out to a daily average of twelve hours per day seven days per week. The Admiral looked at my reported hours and asked, "Have you ever considered giving back half of your pay to the government since you have only worked half the time?" My answer was, "No sir." Fortunately he left it at that.

Admiral Rickover was a brilliant man who demanded a high degree of professionalism and absolute honesty, but he was not without humor. His interviews were unusual. Some were insulting and even bizarre, but I believe that was his plan. Many diesel submarine officers applied for the nuclear power program and many were turned down. These were skilled submariners and proud men who, unfortunately, did not have sufficient engineering background to qualify. If the interviews had been cold and concise it would have crushed the egos of these officers. Instead, stories about the interviews were legendary and each officer that was turned down could talk about that "Crazy Admiral" and not feel the least bit bad about himself. The submarine force needed these officers to return to their diesel boats and to continue their vital service.

After serving on *Gudgeon* for one and a half years and finishing my submarine qualification, I was transferred to Submarine Nuclear Power School in Vallejo, California. Following the academic training in Vallejo, I was sent to the A1W prototype[11] in Idaho where I was finally qualified as an Engineering Officer of the Watch. Having qualified on a

---

[11] A1W was a Westinghouse prototype of the reactor compartment and the after engine room of the USS *Enterprise* (CVN 65).

surface ship prototype I was always concerned that I might be assigned to one. I shouldn't have worried about that as it never became an issue.

U.S. Naval Officers eligible for a nuclear command were trained in the theory and details of the plant equipment and operation and were required to qualify as an Engineering Watch Officer, Engineer Officer, and as a Prospective Commanding Officer of a nuclear powered submarine prior to being assigned as the Commanding Officer. These requirements were established by Admiral Rickover to ensure the safety of the reactor plant.

On the other hand, the Soviet Navy trained their officers in two separate paths: one as a line officer (navigator) seeking command, the second path was designed to prepare an officer for a technical specialty such as Weapons, Electrical, Propulsion (reactor), etc. As a result, the Soviet commanding officer often lacked intimate training and experience on much of the submarine's equipment and was frequently forced to rely on his Department Heads for advice on technical problems.

I met Admiral Rickover many times during my naval career. He interviewed and personally approved of each officer assigned to his U.S. nuclear navy, both surface ship, and submarines. This interview happened several times as a career nuclear officer advanced to command: first when an officer was selected for the nuclear training program; second, when a nuclear officer was tested to qualify as Engineer Officer; and third, when an officer had completed training in Washington, D.C. to become a Commanding Officer.

The Admiral's acceptance was necessary at each step of a nuclear officer's career. Consider the large investment of his time that this required! What CEO of a large company interviews and selects all his management personnel? The Admiral felt that it was imperative that he personally ensured the quality of all officers he was entrusting with the safe operation of a shipboard nuclear power plant. He also embarked on the initial sea trials of each new construction nuclear ship to personally observe the initial testing of the power plant at full power. While on board he directed and observed several training drills by all the engineering watch sections. I can assure you that this was a stress filled event for both officers and crew

CHAPTER IV

ПРЕДВАРИТЕЛЬНО КОМАНД ЛЕТ

(Pre-Command Years)

The years before Alfred Berzin became a fully qualified ship commander were full of training. From 1955 to 1957, he was a commander of the steering group for Whiskey class diesel/electric submarine SSG C 264 in the Baltic Fleet. His group provided submarine design support and logistics for modifications to this class of submarines, and so was in charge of a lot of experimental design changes. From 1959 to 1960, he was put at the disposal of the Commander of Submarine Forces of the Baltic Fleet and made many trips as ship's Navigator on the steamship, *Vasily Kachalov.* Such experience served to enhance and expand his operational and navigational skills. From 1960 to 1961, he was assigned as an Assistant Commander of a Whiskey class diesel/electric submarine SSG C 163 in the Red Banner Baltic Fleet in Ust-Dvinsk.[12] These were years of great learning, both experiential and otherwise. And sometimes that learning was gleaned second hand — as the mistakes of others can provide some of the greatest learning experiences of all.

Captain N[13], a submarine commanding officer and Berzin's su-

---

[12] Ust-Dvinsk is a neighborhood in North West Riga, Latvia.

[13] Captain N is a pseudonym used by Admiral to protect the identity of the officer involved.

perior, told of a Quartermaster who had decided that submariners did not have very good appetites while on patrol. Therefore, the Quartermaster left some of the provisions ashore. Captain N was conducting his first patrol as Commanding Officer, so Rear Admiral Petrov (also a pseudonym), his Division Commander and a great gourmet, was on board to evaluate the captain's performance. The Admiral's wife had given him a special, homemade dish of pork fat with garlic to take to sea and it was stored on board in the officers' wardroom refrigerator. With fifteen days remaining of the patrol, the quartermaster decided to inventory the provisions and the results were shocking! There were only three days of provisions remaining for the last fifteen days onboard. The crew would have to fast or be on short rations.

As this report went from the Quartermaster via the Mate, the Political Officer, and the Commanding Officer, up to the Admiral it became less accurate at every stage. Finally, the Admiral was informed that everything would be fine, only a few, unimportant ingredients were missing. But Rear Admiral Petrov was a wise, old man and he knew perfectly well the art of good reporting, so he decided to call the Quartermaster for a direct report. When Petrov heard that they had only three days of provisions left on board, his anger was like a tsunami and hurricane Clotilda[14] combined. No one was left unscathed!

To add to the Admiral's fury, two wardroom stewards heard the Admiral's conversation with the Quartermaster and understood the consequences that were coming. They quickly finished up the remaining four pounds of Petrov's wife's homemade delicacy. This disappearance was discovered that same day and the Rear Admiral became a complete lunatic. He ran around, shouting complicated curses about the crews' forefathers, who in his opinion were either Neanderthals or ichthyosaurus.

Finally, the three day provision stock was redistributed for fifteen days and every crewman had to be satisfied with only twenty percent of

---

[14] Hurricane Clotilda is the name given to one particularly intense hurricane in Russian history.

the normal, daily ration. Young men, some of whom performed hard, physical work, got only a little piece of bread and a portion of water-like fish soup. All hard jobs and exercises were canceled. The crew only kept watch and additional sleep time was prescribed. After seven days, some sailors became so weak that special levers were needed to help open and close difficult valves.

As the submarine approached the pier at the end of the patrol, slim sailors on deck were reeling in the light wind. Rear Admiral Petrov shouted angrily from the bridge, "Arrest all of the quartermasters and seal up the warehouses!" The ship's Quartermaster was escorted from the submarine under arrest and the provisions left by him ashore were brought on board and given to the crew. After that incident, Rear Admiral Petrov often advised the commanding officers in his division to learn from other's mistakes. He added that only a stupid man learns solely from his own mistakes.

Unfortunately, Captain N did not heed the Admiral's advice. On his next patrol he miscalculated the number of air regeneration aids he would need to complete the patrol. Regeneration aids are containers that hold special plates for oxygen generation and carbon dioxide absorption. The ship ran out of these containers for the last ten days of the patrol, making life unbearable. The Captain was lucky that Rear Admiral Petrov was not on board this time. With no regeneration, the air inside a submarine becomes very bad. An excess of carbon dioxide and lack of oxygen makes people weak, sleepy, and very quickly exhausted. In the old days, submarines had to surface to ventilate. It could be done this time, but then the submarine would be detected by foreign, anti-submarine forces, which is a gross failure on any patrol. In order to avoid being detected, the following solution was proposed: while submerged, the ship's air compressors were run in order to lower the pressure inside the submarine, then the submarine went to periscope depth and the pressure was equalized with the atmosphere through a special tube (snorkel).This procedure drew new air into the submarine and was repeated several times a day during the last ten days. It was a very difficult time. Headaches and breathing difficulties, due to lack of oxygen, were followed by sharp pains in both ears and nose during fast pressure changes in the ship.[15] Once again, lessons were learned.

In 1962, Berzin was transferred to the Pacific Fleet as an Assistant to the Commander of an Echo II class nuclear submarine SSGN K 56 and served in that capacity from 1962 to 1965. During that time he attended the Sixth Higher Special Officer Classes Navy Fleet (command department) in Obninsk[16] and graduated with the specialty of a "Commander of a Submarine." (This training was similar to the U.S. Navy's Submarine Prospective Commanding Officers course).

From 1965 to 1969, he served as Executive Officer of Echo II class, nuclear submarine SSGN K 31 in the Pacific Fleet, not unlike that which we would trail during May 1972. During that time, a local officer of the Committee for State Security (KGB) decided to check out the vigilance of the local submarine force security. The KGB officer made an I.D. badge with the photo of a dog. He passed successfully through several checkpoints and even managed to board a submarine which was preparing to go to sea. The officer then went to the reactor control panel and started randomly pressing buttons. Only at this point was he discovered. A lot of officials were punished for the incident and even though it did not occur on Berzin's submarine, everyone felt the security repercussions.

There are many possible hazards on a submarine, which is why there are extensive training and a significant number of rules. The following incident occurred in 1968 — a reminder of why there are so many rules in place. A submarine was being repaired at the nearby

---

[15] This practice of lowering the air pressure and equalizing through the snorkel mast was also frequently used by U.S. diesel submarines. It wasn't until the early 1960s that this practice was discredited. Lowering the air pressure in the submarine resulted in less oxygen for the crew, a condition not unlike mountain climbers at high altitude struggling to get their breathe. When you equalize with the atmosphere you were just getting back the oxygen you would have had all along. Nothing was gained.

[16] Obninsk is one of the major Russian science cities and included a training base for the crew of the Soviet Union's first nuclear submarine, the *Leninsky Komsomol*, or K 3. Now the city is home to twelve scientific institutes. Their main activities are nuclear power engineering, radiation technology, and meteorology.

factory (shipyard). The working day was about to end and a new watch team was supposed to come relieve the current watch. Lieutenant Commander Dubov was on duty and he had arranged to meet with the new Duty Officer, First Lieutenant Kaplanov, at the plant's security checkpoint. This arrangement of relieving the off going Duty Officer of his responsibilities at the gate and not on the submarine was a serious violation of regulations because a Duty Officer was required to be on the submarine at all times. Dubov was in a hurry to get home to prepare for a hunting trip that was happening the following day, so he was impatiently waiting for Kaplanov at the security checkpoint, leaving the submarine watch without a supervisor.

At this time a sailor named Pupkin had finished cleaning the 9th compartment, collected the garbage in a pile, and then should have climbed the ladder to throw the garbage into a trash can on the pier. Pupkin was too lazy, but he was a resourceful idler, so he walked to the DDC device and decided to throw trash through it. The DDC is only meant to be used at sea while submerged. It is a short tube in the pressure shell and has two lids, one of them is on the outside and opens to the sea and one is inside of the compartment. It also has an interlock system to prevent both lids from being opened simultaneously. Why? In order not to sink the submarine. But the boat was being repaired, including the DDC and there was a sign on the inner lid cautioning, "Do not open!" Despite this warning, Pupkin opened the lid into the compartment, put in the garbage, and then opened the lid connecting to the sea without closing the inner lid. Water gushed into the compartment. Pupkin got scared and ran away from the compartment, but fortunately another crew member declared an emergency situation, sealed the compartment, and pressurized it using high pressure air, saving the submarine from sinking! As the scene unfolded, the new Duty Officer, Kaplanov, appeared on the horizon. His first sight was of rushing emergency teams from other submarines heading for the ship he was supposed to be watching.

A very tense debriefing with the Brigade Commander happened the following day and everyone was punished severely. For their edification they were declared cretins and ichthyosaurs. Of course the process of selecting men to serve on submarines is very strict, as it should be, but even then incidents continue to happen.

MINTON'S PRE-COMMAND YEARS

In January 1962, I reported to the Blue Crew of USS *Thomas Jefferson* (SSBN 618) being built at Newport News Shipyard, Virginia. I first served as the Auxiliary Division Officer and then the Main Propulsion Assistant throughout the construction period and sea trials, and made her initial Polaris Patrol. Ballistic missile submarines went on deterrent patrols during the Cold War during which they were in constant communication to immediately strike targets if necessary. At the end of that patrol, Bill Hobler, the Electrical Officer, and I returned to Washington, D.C. to take the Engineer Officer Examination. The exam was an extremely long, eight hours, and difficult. I used the complete allotted time, including the breaks, but still ran out of time. During the last section of the exam, I just listed the major factors/issues and did not completely answer any question. Bill finished the exam early and, when we met afterward, was confident that he had passed. I was sure that I had failed. The next day we had our interviews with Admiral Rickover. Soon after returning to our off-crew office in New London, Connecticut, I was surprised and pleased to find out that I had passed the exam; unfortunately Bill had not and had to return for a second exam.

After the *Jefferson,* I was assigned back to Newport News Shipyard for a second new construction as Engineer Officer of the USS *Sam Rayburn* (Gold) (SSBN 635). I served in that capacity through the construction period and two Polaris Patrols.

In June 1966, I was assigned to the Fleet Submarine Training Facility (FSTF) in Pearl Harbor, Hawaii, as Officer in charge of the Engineering Training Department. While at FSTF I was able to construct the first Submarine "Get Wet" Damage Control Trainer using salvaged equipment and a few night requisitions from the Pearl Harbor Naval Shipyard. Also during this period, I finished my command thesis, attended the Prospective Commanding Officer School as a Prospective Executive Officer, and completed my operational qualification for submarine command. I still needed to attend the Admiral

Rickover Pre-Command School in Washington, D.C., often referred to as "charm school," but that training and exam would come after my Executive Officer tour.

I reported to the USS *Swordfish* (SSN 579) in Hong Kong and relieved the Executive Officer while we transited to Sasebo, Japan for an eight day refit. In Sasebo the *Swordfish* was moored alongside a surface ship tender anchored in the harbor to complete last minute repairs on some sensitive equipment and to provide rest and relaxation for the officers and crew prior to commencing a special operation.

During the preparation for this deployment, I was approached by one of our engineering Chief Petty Officers who told me he was concerned about the provisions being loaded for our upcoming deployment — this is going to sound very familiar. He said that previously when provisions were loaded, the spaces outboard of the two, main condensers had been completely filled with cans of coffee. This time there was almost nothing being loaded in those spaces. I went to the Supply Officer and had him conduct an inventory of the amount of coffee on board. Much to his surprise there was about half of the required amount. The Chief Petty Officer had saved us from a major morale problem. I cannot imagine running out of coffee during a patrol. Coffee held us together during those long days at sea.

The Japanese were always suspicious of nuclear submarines in their ports and anti-nuclear activists continuously patrolled the water around our boat. On May 6, 1968, a water sample taken near us had a fleeting indication on their radiation meter and the activists immediately reported this event as proof that we were contaminating the harbor. The fact that they were not set up to capture the water running through their instrument and were not ever able to duplicate the reading was ignored. The most likely cause for the meter's signal fluctuation was electronic interference by one of the numerous shipboard radars in the harbor. The results of their report caused little concern in the local press. The harbor was a cesspool that was far more dangerous to the public than any imaginary indication of radioactive contamination. The initial, public reaction in Sasebo was low-keyed and despite the activists trying to drum up a larger response, there was only one, short demonstration while we were in port. The base security allowed this demonstration to march down to the fleet landing under security's control. I found it hilarious that one of our petty officers, temporarily assigned to the shore patrol, was in front of the demonstration leading them to the landing. He was, of course, in uniform wearing his submarine dolphins. Fortunately it was raining lightly and his raincoat covered up his dolphin pin, so the demonstrators didn't know he was from the submarine.

During that same time, the reaction in Tokyo was much larger and soon became a serious political issue. Because of additional equipment problems, our stay in Sasebo had been extended two more days which did not help calm the Japanese reaction. In the evening of the second day, I received a message that we were to get underway and leave Sasebo as soon as possible. The message ended with the phrase "Dean Rusk sends."[17] We knew then we had really stirred up a hornet's nest by being there. I contacted the Captain, Commander Taylor Rigsbee, and told him that we were being thrown out of port the next morning. We got underway as ordered; flying a giant carp flag from our mast in celebration of Boy's Day [18] and to acknowledge the hospitality the city had given us during our stay. I have always wondered how the Japanese press managed to remove the carp from their pictures of the "bad" submarine leaving their port.

Although submarine operations are dangerous, the officers and crew are generally good humored and often kid each other and play jokes on their shipmates. The following shipboard hoax is one of the more elaborate examples of this game playing and our sense of humor.

So off we went on a special operation and began to settle into our underway routine. The ship had a newspaper which took news off the radio teletype printout when time permitted. This news was augmented by shipboard news written by various crew members and often contained teasing about each other's mistakes and foibles. The Engineer Officer, Lieutenant Commander Richard (Dick) Lee, was in

---

[17] David Dean Rusk was the Unites States Secretary of State from 1961 to 1969 under presidents John F. Kennedy and Lyndon B. Johnson.

[18] On Boy's Day Japanese families raise a carp-shaped flag for each boy. Legend has it when a carp swims upstream it becomes a dragon, and the way the flags blow in the wind looks like they are swimming.

charge of the newspaper and came to me with an idea for a hoax that he could run in the paper during the patrol. It sounded like fun and would get a good laugh once the patrol was over. The only person on board that was in on the hoax beside Dick and I was the Chief Radioman. He would stop the teletype and insert the news with appropriate typo errors that were common in all teletype transmission these reports were spaced out on a timeline as the false timeline was played out. We even left the skipper out of the know.

When you control the only source of outside news, almost anything goes. The hoax was a report of a Soviet spaceship launch to the moon and its safe return to earth. The scenario was fairly elaborate and as you will see, turned out to be very convincing. The timing was critical to the overall effect since this story started in mid-May, 1968, and the space race with the Soviet Union was in full throttle.

The first human spaceflight had taken place on April 12, 1961, when cosmonaut Yuri Gagarin made one orbit around the Earth aboard the *Vostok 1* spacecraft. The United States became the second nation to achieve manned spaceflight, with the suborbital flight of astronaut Alan Shepard aboard *Mercury 7* on May 5, 1961. On May 25, 1961, President Kennedy announced his support of the *Apollo* program and defined the ultimate goal of the Space Race was to land a man on the moon and return him safely to the earth before this decade was over. In 1968, when we went on patrol, that goal had not yet been achieved. It wasn't until July 20, 1969, that Neil Armstrong and Buzz Aldrin became the first humans to set foot on the moon, so our hoax had perfect timing. The first news reports were as follows:

> *"The world's largest spacecraft, Cosmos IX, was on schedule and the mission was going as planned." Sunday TASS headlined the entire first page covering the latest Russian space spectacular. Unofficial sources in Moscow say the payload of the huge rocket was in the neighborhood of seventy thousand pounds.*
>
> *In a separate article NASA officials stated, that if the reports from Moscow can be certified, the U.S. has fallen behind in the development of rockets capable of*

sending a man to the moon, as had been tentatively
planned for late this year.

Dr. William Von Escher, head of the rocket labora-
tory at Cape Kennedy, stated Monday, "The U.S. has
nothing in its rocket arsenal that could at this time put
a seventy thousand pound payload into space."

With the hoax in automatic, the patrol went on. I was busy standing Command Duty watch and writing the patrol report, I simply forgot about it. Meanwhile, the situation in Japan over the *Swordfish's* alleged discharge incident continued to heat up. The Japanese Premier, Eisaku Sato, closed all Japanese ports to U.S. nuclear powered ships and our government agreed to an immediate investigation of the allegations. This resulted in *Swordfish* being called off the special operation and an inspection team, made up of one Naval Reactors representative and two Operational Reactors Safety Examining Board (ORSE) members, being helicoptered on board. With the team onboard, *Swordfish* was ordered to transit to Guam. The inspectors went to work right away reviewing all our records, procedures, and operator training. Officers and crew members responsible for the plant operation during our stay in Sasebo were interviewed extensively.

While this inspection was being conducted, the hoax continued unabated with the following reports over several days:

"An article from the British Observatory in London is-
sued a statement saying, 'It is very possible that Cosmos
IX, the latest Russian moon rocket, may be manned.'
The spokesman for the observatory also added that
tapes from radio signals from the spacecraft indicate
that the Russians seem to be using a scrambled signal
similar to that used by the military when holding high
level conferences by radio telephone. To back up his
statement, he noted that the Russian ground stations
have been sending more signals to this spacecraft than
in the case of any other previous Russian space probes;
also the pauses between ground and space signals show

that one transmission seems to wait for a reply from the other.

NASA officials in Washington would not confirm or deny the British speculation concerning the possibility of a manned Russian lunar probe. Unofficially NASA officials are saying Russia is known to hold back on confirmation of its rocket flights until they are a proven success; speculation continues even here, that this could well be the first manned flight to the moon. NASA discounts any reports that the Russians are ready to attempt any landing on the moon's surface, saying that several more experimental flights are required before any country is ready for such a feat.

Moscow (UPI) — Colonel Alexandre Malenkov and Major Mikol Schelesnaya are safely on their way back to earth. The two cosmonauts in Cosmos IX blasted off the moon's surface right on schedule. Russian scientist, Colonel Malenkov, pressed the button to ignite the rockets that lifted them off the moon at exactly 10:43 p.m. (GMT). Malenkov reported that the rockets had fired and they were lifting off. Five minutes later he reported that Cosmos IX had left the moon and their altitude was presently 165,000 feet from the moon, and he was preparing to maneuver the spaceship for the journey that would carry them back to Russia. A bulletin issued at 10:00 p.m. (GMT) said preliminary maneuvers had been made successfully and the two cosmonauts could relax now for at least twenty-four hours. At that time, a delicate midcourse maneuver halfway back to Earth was to be made. Russian scientists say that if they missed, they could sail off the horizon and permanently orbit around the sun. TASS defined the accuracy needed as being fantastic. It will be like William Tell trying to shoot an apple off the boy's head at 1000 feet." Russian scientists are not talking about missing. In fact they say they are absolutely confident Cosmos IX will land on schedule.

Moscow (UPI) —the Russian news agency TASS reported today that all is going well aboard Cosmos IX and the two cosmonauts were resting in preparation for their final maneuver prior to landing. TASS stated that radio communications deteriorated somewhat during the night, but both cosmonauts seem to be resting fitfully. A spokesman for the news agency reported that Cosmos IX was proceeding through space on schedule. This would mean the rocket would land Thursday and the cosmonauts would be honored in Red Square sometime that afternoon. Even before the cosmonauts are safely on the ground, invitations for the two, Russian heroes are arriving from capitals all over the world. TASS said the two spacemen would make a tour of a few selected countries."

You can tell that the details we used for the hoax made it seem legitimate. We tried to have various points of view to give it realism. The reports continued, including the following excerpts:

"Washington —All across the nation, people are divided today on the Russian space success. Some people say the Russians are to be congratulated, others are a little angry. As one man in New York City put it, 'With all of the money our government has put into the space program, I find it hard to believe another country beat us to the moon.' Some Senators and Congressmen are already looking for someone to take the blame for the Russians beating us to the moon. But, the most disappointed people in the U.S. today are the astronauts who have been training for the first flight to the moon.

Moscow UPI - TASS, the official Russian news agency, announced this morning the safe return of Cosmos IX and cosmonauts, Colonel Alexandre

Malenkov and Major Mikol Schelesnaya. The two cosmonauts guided their spacecraft to earth at 11:53 p.m. GMT near the city of Omsk in the central plains area of Russia. The two, Russian heroes were greeted by Premier Alexei Kosygin and many other leading Communists. TASS described the event as one of happiness and joy. The two are to spend three to four hours with Russian, space scientists, particular attention being given to Schelesnaya, who became the first human to step on the surface of another planet. He spent fifteen minutes outside the Cosmos IX while the spacecraft was on the moon. No western newsmen were allowed to view the landing; however, they will be able to attend a news conference with the two cosmonauts sometime later. The Russians announced they will share with the world the scientific knowledge gained from, what TASS headlined as, the greatest achievement in the history of mankind. The two cosmonauts were described in excellent health and bursting with joy and pride.

TASS said that on their return to earth, Malenkov was the first cosmonaut to step out from the spacecraft. He was immediately embraced by Premier Kosygin. Also, with the Premier were Malenkov's wife and four children. Schelesnaya stepped out seconds later and, he too received a warm embrace from the Premier. The proud parents of both cosmonauts were also present. TASS said the two cosmonauts spent fifteen minutes with their families and then were whisked off for debriefing with the scientists."

Our hoax finally ended with the full text of a letter from President Lyndon Johnson congratulating the Russian people for their spectacular achievement. It was a little bittersweet. We had lost the race.

During the transit to Guam, the visiting inspection team got into heated debates with our Captain, Commander Taylor Rigsbee, about why the U.S. could not beat the Russians. Periodically I would egg them on, but it was hard for Dick and me to keep straight faces. I remember the Captain's reaction when the Russians first reported the successful landing of the Cosmos IX. He slammed his fist on the table and said, "Can't we do anything right!" The whole crew was up in arms about the Russians beating us to the moon.

The inspection team finished their assessment just before we reached Guam. They certified to the Commander of the U.S. Pacific Fleet and Admiral Rickover, that the *Swordfish* had not discharged radioactive coolant into Sasebo harbor. The team left the ship immediately upon arrival in Guam. Neither Dick Lee nor I remembered to let them know that the Russian, space story was a hoax.

Of course the story wasn't quite over; someone had to tell the Captain, so I elected Dick to tell him. Dick, with some trepidation, went into the Captain's cabin and gave him a whole accounting of the hoax. The Captain thought for a minute and then said with a smile, "What a great yarn!"

The two ORSE Board members had been traveling so much, the fact that they hadn't heard reports of Russian space activity before transferring aboard *Swordfish* didn't seem strange. Dick learned later that when they arrived back in Hawaii they talked about it to other people for a (very short) time. Soon they stopped mentioning it, even to each other. It must have been embarrassing to certify that *Swordfish* had not discharged radioactive coolant into Sasebo harbor, but had completely tricked them into thinking that the Russians had successfully gone to the moon. Despite the team's gullibility, the report stood and the Japanese opened their ports to nuclear ships a year later. *Swordfish* was one of the first to make a return visit to Yokosuka, Japan.

One final incident came from this hoax. A *Swordfish* sailor had written to his mother about the Russian moon shot during the transit and the letter got off of the ship in Guam before the hoax was announced to the crew. His mother was so incensed about our government keeping the news secret from the American public that she wrote her Congressman. Fortunately this issue died a quick death and did not become a problem.

During my second deployment on *Swordfish* we tapped the sea bottom while turning south at the eastern end of the Tsugaru Strait off of Japan. An unusual vibration was felt throughout the boat while on our submerged passage of the strait. With *Swordfish's* wardroom and officer's staterooms just forward of the control room, I was immediately in the control room and ordered a "Jump-Fifty." This was a unique procedure we had developed as a safety measure when we were operating close to the ocean floor. It enabled us to decrease the submarine's depth by fifty feet almost immediately. The Jump-Fifty procedure consisted of a short, emergency, ballast tank blow followed by opening the main, ballast tank vents. The air entered all ballast tanks simultaneously and moved the submarine up on a level keel and opening the ballast tank vents quickly stopped this rise. It was important for the submarine to come up level because any up angle used to change depth would first push the stern deeper toward the bottom. The Officer of the Deck then changed course to the left and decreased depth an additional hundred feet. I had a sounding taken which showed us at a safe depth and announced to the control room that we must have contacted some floating debris or wreck near the bottom. That was the way it was entered into the ship's log. The Commanding Officer accepted this explanation and the event was nearly forgotten.

When we entered our next port, Yokosuka, Japan, our divers inspected the underwater portion of the hull, finding only one discrepancy. The mine clearing pad on the lower section of our rudder was missing.[19] The repair yard in Yokosuka made a replacement and divers replaced the missing pad; all is well that ends well. We will never know what we hit, but the lesson was clear, we were operating too deep for no good reason. It pays to be conservative when there is no return for being daring.

When *Swordfish* returned to Pearl Harbor from this six month deployment in the Western Pacific, we had a little problem with the Naval Reactors (NR) representative. The NR representative arrived late in the evening after *Swordfish* had entered port to monitor the shut-down

---

[19] The fittings to attach mine clearing cables to guide moored mines away from the Submarine hull were a left over from the experiences of World War II. Needless to say these were not used during the Cold War, but the attachments were still part of *Swordfish's* design.

activities of the engineering department. These representatives were similar to Soviet Political Officers, in that they were not in our chain of command. They reported directly to Admiral Rickover and because of this relationship, they were threatening and their visits were always a cause for concern.

On this occasion, the NR representative did not report to the topside watch (security guard) and went straight down the hatch into the submarine, without permission. The topside watch passed the word, "Intruder on board." The representative was quickly found and escorted to the Duty Officer, Lieutenant Commander Dick Lee. He questioned the representative and determined that he had not asked for, or been given permission to come aboard. In addition, his identification badge was damaged and possibly tampered with, so the Duty Officer telephoned the local NR office. When he was satisfied that the representative was authorized to make the visit, the representative believed he would be allowed to inspect the engineering spaces, but this was not the case. The Duty Officer directed the representative to leave the ship and told him that he could not return until he learned how to properly board a U.S. submarine and had obtained a proper security badge.

Lieutenant Commander Lee then called our Commanding Officer and the Squadron Commander's Duty Officer. Everyone was afraid that his actions could lead to serious repercussions, but this did not happen. The Officer-in-Charge of the Naval Reactors Office in Honolulu knew that if the event was reported to Admiral Rickover, the NR office would have been faulted, not *Swordfish*. We were pleased that we had been spared the wrath of the Admiral.

CHAPTER V

РАННИЕ КОМАНД ЛЕТ

(Early Command Years)

Commander Berzin's assignment to the Echo II class SSGN K 184 occurred in 1969 when he was assigned to the 26th Division of Soviet Submarines in the Red Banner Pacific Fleet during the submarine's overhaul. Although this command tour was initially expected to be temporary, it continued as a full tour from 1969 to 1974.

The Echo II class, nuclear powered cruise-missile submarines, carried the front series of radars that enabled them to launch the anti-shipping version of the Shaddock missile. These were primarily anti-carrier weapons, intended originally as a response to potential nuclear strikes against the Soviet Union. These missiles came in both nuclear and conventional versions.

When K 184's overhaul was finally completed, the crew began regular duties and the dockside trials were started. At the pier, representatives from the factory[20], military staff, and submarine personnel participated in the tests of all submarine mechanisms.

After the dockside trials, the submarine started running trials at sea to ensure all systems were running properly. This was Berzin's first time at sea as the commanding officer. After completing the sea trials, the factory started to correct the identified machinery, systems, and

---

[20] In Russia shipyards were referred to as a "factory".

equipment problems. The driving force in solving many problems was "awl," which was nothing more than technical alcohol (ethanol). The submariners and factory workers loved awl; it was a kind of currency. It was also used for electrical equipment cleaning. To complete a submarine overhaul, the submarine received one hundred liters of this alcohol. To prevent people from drinking it, the alcohol was passed through a gasoline hose, but this was not a significant enough obstacle. People who drank this had gasoline burps, but they continued to drink the awl anyway. One of the nicknames given to awl was benzolikerchik (gasoline-liquor).

From September 24 to October 5, 1971, K 184 put to sea to conduct a training search operation in the Sea of Okhotsk, searching for the "blue" submarine but instead encountered a nightmare.

At 12:30 p.m. on September 29, while operating at a depth of eighty meters, there was a release of radioactive gas in the forward equipment space of the 6th (reactor) compartment. The radioactive gas and aerosol readings quickly increased in the forward equipment space to twenty times the normal allowable limit on the second and third levels of the compartment. The signal and announcement of "radioactive danger" was given immediately and a special emergency zone was declared in the 5th, 6th, and 7th compartments. The Engineer Officer, Captain Second Rank Bayburin, and the Chemical Defense Officer, Captain Third Rank Yagoshin, reported the conditions and recommended a course of action. Berzin decided to surface and ventilate the 6th compartment to the open air and within ten minutes the submarine had surfaced and had begun the ventilation. Literally two minutes later, electronic countermeasures detected a AN/APS-80 radar and an American P-3 Orion aircraft appeared out of the clouds and began to fly over at an altitude of one hundred meters.

Avoiding detection being a priority, K 184 altered course, commenced an emergency dive and cleared the area by twenty miles. By this time the situation with regards to the gas and aerosol radioactivity was more complicated. It was now three hundred times allowable levels on the third deck in the 6th compartment and five thousand times the allowable limit in the forward equipment space. On the second deck, it was seventeen hundred times the limit and in the 5th and 7th compartments it was around forty times. To leave personnel in these compartments was no longer possible. All unnecessary personnel were removed from the affected compartments and a message was sent to the base detailing the deteriorating situation.

In the 5th, 6th, and 7th compartments, the level of contamination reached one hundred counts/minute and were shut down so they could be ventilated them to the atmosphere. By midnight on September 29, the levels in the 5th and 7th compartments were down to normal and in the 6th compartment they were down to just one to two times the allowable levels. Yet, by this time, radioactive levels had reached five to ten times the norm in all other compartments. By noon on September 30, the situation on board had stabilized. The gas and aerosol levels throughout the boat fell to normal levels. Captain Second Rank Bayburin and Captain Third Rank Yagoshin reported that the cause for the radiation leak was the cover of the reactor vessel. Berzin again sent a message to shore reporting the condition and asking for permission to return to base. Once granted, the submarine headed for home. Some of the crew suffered headaches, chest pains, and fatigue that didn't go away for a month.

The consequences of the exposure only began to appear much later. The actual doses received by the crew members were hidden from the commander and staff, and the doctors did not link this exposure to subsequent illnesses. Fairly young sailors, Voronin and Tsimbalenko, later died and the cause was written off due to other ailments—according to the oncologists, their deaths were a result of pre-cancerous conditions.

Surface decontamination was conducted onboard for a long time with little effect. The training accident continued to haunt Commander Berzin, who would spend several decades trying to get remuneration for his crew for the contamination they suffered.

====

Back at sea, Berzin once again began a patrol. Onboard was Rear Admiral Hitrenko, who was evaluating whether Captain Berzin was qualified to make independent patrols as the commanding officer.

This was not a whim of the Admiral's, this was a standard procedure established by the Chief of the Soviet Navy. Berzin had recently been transferred from the submarine. These forces consist of surface ships, submarines, aircraft, training center and the previous commander of the submarine, Captain Second Rank Sobachevsky, was transferred ashore having been elected as a delegate to the 24th Congress of the Communist Party.

Prior to this patrol, while conducting underway training, another significant accident occurred. The submarine was at a depth of one hundred meters and at a speed of twenty knots. Due to a sudden malfunction, the hydroplanes jammed at fifteen degrees dive and the submarine quickly pitched down by the bow and sank to a depth close to its depth limit. Further increase in the depth would have led to the destruction of the pressure hull and to the submarine's demise. Berzin kept his head; he stood by and evaluated everything as it was happening and had only one thought, "Get out of this situation!" A pale faced, boatswain mate was operating the hydroplanes and he did his best to trim the ship using the stern planes. The Diving Officer ordered a high pressure air blow into the bow and the main group of ballast tanks. This time fate had released them. All of the actions took only fifty-five seconds and saved the lives of everyone onboard. As a result of this accident during training, the Captain was constantly in the control room, where the entire submarine could be managed. There was a cabin in another compartment for him, but after using it once, he did not use it again. Instead, he had a temporary bed of planks and boxes with a mattress, blanket, and pillow built in the control room. He slept with one ear open to hear everything. If there was the slightest problem at night, he was able to get up immediately.

The situation handled, Berzin quickly moved to current affairs and concerns. In a few hours they were to ascend to periscope depth to receive a radio broadcast from the base. He summoned the Chief Mate and together they discussed how best to perform this maneuver. When they finished talking, he looked at his watch. It was ten minutes before the ascent. Berzin sounded the General Quarters alarm. The sharp sound of a howler filled the compartments. The crew rushed to their battle stations and reported on alert. The hydrophone operators listened to the aquatic environment. When they did not detect any surface ships and vessels they reported, "The horizon is clear." This meant the sonar horizon was clear. Only after the submarine ascended to a periscope depth, the periscope had been raised, and the Commanding Officer did not see any contacts on the horizon or in the air, was the order given to write in the log, "The horizon is clear." Then an antenna for receiving radio and radar signals was raised. As submariners say, a "communication session" began. A few minutes later the radio operator reported to the commander, "All messages addressed to us have been received, the session is over." The commander gave the order to lower all masts and to dive to a depth of eighty meters.

After this session Rear Admiral Hitrenko invited Berzin to go to the chart room where he took out his notebook. Looking at it he began listing his comments, "Ascent to periscope depth was poorly organized, your watchstanders suffer from verbal diarrhea and a lot of them chattered profusely. You should clearly command and receive reports. Before the ascent the boat was not ready, part of the crew continued to doze off while in combat positions. I ask you to toughen your demands on your people." In fact, of course, Hitrenko's comments were valid.

Two days later the submarine was to pass through the strait between two islands into the open ocean. While operating independently, the Commanding Officer must constantly bear in mind navigational safety. He needs to know with precision the position of his submarine. This is necessary to avoid running aground, collision with reefs, islands, coastlines, and with other ships. Therefore the Navigator, whenever possible, must determine their position, using all technical means available, including sonar and radar. The use of active sonar and radar may allow foreign anti-submarine forces to use space vehicles and stationary sonar arrays.

In peacetime, the Americans demonstrated great skill in covertly tracking the Soviets. Unwittingly the fleet staff had been a great help to these forces by setting a pattern of using the same routes each year. Soviet staff officers clearly did not shine at military strategy. While submerged, the submarine becomes nearly invisible, this stealth feature is the advantage that allows a submarine to torpedo or make a surprise missile attack which may eventually allow them to win over a more powerful enemy. Choosing between navigational safety and stealth, the Commanding Officer must exercise a certain art and find a balanced solution. Two years earlier the previous Commanding Officer, Captain Second Rank Sobachevsky, on his first patrol was given the same route. Senior Deputy Squadron Commander, Vorobyov, a man with great conceit, on the first day of the patrol banned the commander from the use of active sonar and radar. Sobachevsky did not contradict him, and to complicate the situation, he decided to approach the Strait at a slow speed quiet condition so that the foreign anti-submarine forces could not detect them. He planned to fix the submarine's position by celestial bodies and foreign radio navigation systems.

As it turned out, the Navigator had a pretty mediocre theoretical knowledge of radio navigation and little practical experience in its use. The sky was completely overcast eliminating the possibility of using stars to determine their exact location. In addition the Navigator, because of negligence, did not properly take into account the Kuro – Siwo current which reaches speeds in places of two or more knots. All this led to a significant error in determining their location. Both Vorobyov and Sobachevsky should have monitored the work of the Navigator more closely, but they did not. As a result, the nuclear submarine carrying nuclear and conventional weapons, instead of approaching the Strait was approaching the island of Okinawa. No one in the crew knew or felt the impending danger. The submarine was only saved by its slow speed. At once, in all of the compartments of the submarine, they heard a loud screeching and grinding. The submarine ascended to a depth of forty meters, after ten minutes the grinding was repeated. After that, the submarine ascended to periscope depth. Sobachevsky saw through the periscope directly on their course a beach where people were sunbathing and on the left and right were visible rocks. The commander reversed course and brought the submarine into deeper water. The location error was determined to be forty miles (seventy-four kilometers). Comments, as they say, are irrelevant. This case was entered into the history of Soviet submarining. For many years, it was taught in schools, academies, and fleets as a vivid example of human carelessness, stupidity, and irresponsibility.

After the communications session, the commander of electronic intelligence came to Berzin. He reported the interception of a radio message from a U.S. anti-submarine "Orion" aircraft. The report alerted the Commanding Officer and his first thought was, "Did he detect us?" He was well familiar with this potential enemy. In the past, Orion aircraft had successfully detected and monitored Soviet submarines. The aircraft has radar, a magnetic anomaly detector, electronic intercept equipment, and sonar buoys which can be dropped into the water to listen for submarines and transmit their sounds to the aircraft. In wartime, the "Orion" aircraft was capable of using torpedoes and bombs, including those with nuclear warheads. In the end, Berzin analyzed the situation and concluded that the plane was searching at a distance of one hundred fifty miles from the submarine and was not a threat.

At 8:00 p.m. when the submarine next ascended to periscope depth for a communications session from the base, they received a report of a U.S. Naval exercise in the immediate vicinity of their route, followed by the coordinates, course, and speed of the aircraft carrier *Ticonderoga* and her four escorts. Fleet headquarters ordered them to close the aircraft carrier and increase their frequency of communication session to every four hours. The purpose of this guidance was to assist the submarine in making sonar contact with the aircraft carrier. In time of peace they would track the carrier. In time of war they would launch rockets or torpedoes. He began to calculate the course necessary to establish sonar contact with the aircraft carrier. His plan required them to dive to a depth of one hundred sixty meters, increase speed to nineteen knots, and steer a course of 120 degrees.

He gave the necessary commands to execute his plan. At nineteen knots the submarine is very noisy and loses its main tactical feature of secrecy. The American submariners called this kind of maneuver the "roaring cow." He knew and understood, but there was nothing he could do, but obey Fleet headquarters' orders. By the time he had finished his calculations Hitrenko had begun to compare his own results with those of the Berzin and they differed. Without understanding and without checking, Hitrenko immediately began to accuse him of illiteracy. Five minutes later the Navigator also finished checking the calculations and found Hitrenko's mistake. Of course, Hitrenko did not apologize before the personnel on watch. Berzin looked at his watch;

it showed 9:00 p.m., three hours before the next ascent, so he decided to get a little rest. For the past few days he had only slept in fits and starts, but sleep did not come because he was bothered by a headache. He understood that part of it was the air, which of course, was different from the normal atmosphere even though the air regeneration system was operating normally. It was clear that the crew had also begun to tire faster. Resentment of Hitrenko slowly faded imperceptibly and he fell asleep. The mate woke him up at 11:30 p.m. and reported to him softly, "Comrade Commander, there is ten minutes until the scheduled ascent to periscope depth."

At 12:00 a.m. the submarine ascended again for a communication session. The next position of the aircraft carrier *Ticonderoga* was reported by radio. From the electronics intercept station he received the report, "A faint radar signal from an Orion aircraft has been detected at 090 degrees." Maybe the aircraft is looking in our area? In this situation it was impossible for the commander to guess. Had they been detected or had they not been detected? In this situation a submarine has only one solution. They must immediately try to break contact. Therefore, he gave the command to dive and evade. "Set the course of 135 degrees, depth of two hundred twenty meters." With a little delay Hitrenko ordered the commander, "Set the course of 020 degrees, depth of one hundred twenty meters!" In the control room was an uneasy state of confusion, as if a person at the same time received orders to turn both left and right. The confrontation was saved by Berzin who said, "Write in the logbook Rear Admiral Hitrenko has assumed command of the submarine." Hitrenko looked surprised at the Commanding Officer and told him to go to the chart room. Where, being irritated, he asked the following question, "Did you decide to make a fool out of me?" Berzin calmly replied. "That is not the case. In accordance with the regulations of the ship you should not interfere in the management of the submarine." Hitrenko paled with anger and plunged a compass into the chart.

At 4:00 a.m. the communication session provided a new location for the carrier *Ticonderoga*, with four destroyers, and a support ship. They were slowly and surely approaching the submarine. But the Americans had turned off their radio navigation systems, "Loran

Alpha and Charlie," which the Soviet submarine had been successfully using to determine their location. Now the Navigator had only celestial navigation to determine his position and this was often delayed by clouds. Radar in this area was useless for navigation because they were out of range of land.

The communication session ended, the submarine dove to an operating depth and continued to run at nineteen knots. Berzin slept to somewhere around 6:00 a.m. At the 8:00 a.m. communication session, he received another position for the *Ticonderoga*. The electronic countermeasures station detected a radio beacon from the carrier bearing of 70 degrees, at a frequency of 520 kilohertz using a call sign "ON." Detection of the aircraft carrier was immediately reported to the base by radio. The submarine dove, again and again, set a speed of nineteen knots. Berzin slept only two hours that night.

The 12:00 p.m. communication session contained an order from the Navy staff, "Simulate a training missile strike on the aircraft carrier *Ticonderoga*, bearing 300 degrees, speed twenty knots, latitude, and longitude." The fleet commander's radio message was a combat order, which the commander must carry out as soon as possible. The word "training" means that the military rockets are not actually started, but all other actions should be as in war. While at sea, the Commanding Officer decides independently on each combat order. He assesses the situation, makes the necessary calculations, considers the options, and selects the most profitable actions. He then assigns tasks to his subordinates and they must aggressively implement his decision to achieve success and victory over the enemy. Berzin ordered on the ship broadcasting system "Set ship's combat readiness number one." For this, the control room team quickly gathered and he read the military order directing them to conduct a simulated missile launch. This was more than his crew needed because everyone knew what to do and how to do it after many years of service and daily training. In a few minutes the calculations were completed and the information plotted. The Weapons Officer reported readiness for pre-launch preparation. Berzin checked the calculations on the chart and gave the command, "This is a drill, man battle stations." A shrill howler was heard in all compartments. The crew began to take their posts. A minute later the mate reported that the submarine was ready to fight. After that, he gave the order: "Missile attack, begin pre-launch preparation." The Weapons Officer ordered the programming of the missile with the position of the aircraft carrier *Ticonderoga* and its course and speed. Missiles in the steel containers came alive. Although their rocket motors were blocked, through the wires into their brains ran the information about the enemy. In a few minutes they would have to find the carrier in the ocean and destroy it. Having completed the pre-launch, the Weapons Officer reported to the Commanding Officer, "Rocket launch warmed up, ready to surface."

The submarine was brought to periscope depth and the horizon was checked clear. Berzin gave the order, "Surface, Blow Main Ballast. Containers up!" The submarine surfaced and the containers were slowly raised into the vast blue sky with no clouds above a calm dark ocean. They simulated a launch of conventional missiles. Radio immediately reported to the base that they had simulated a strike on the aircraft carrier. At that point, the electronic countermeasures station reported, "Detected radar signal from an Orion bearing left ten degrees." This aircraft could easily detect a submarine on the surface, and if this happens, they would be able to attack in eight to ten minutes. Berzin gave the command, "Emergency dive!" The submarine dove to a safe depth and began evasive maneuvers.

Today submarines can launch missiles from underwater, but in those days they could not. When a submarine surfaced to launch it lost its secrecy and became a very easy target. According to Soviet belief, the Americans never built submarines requiring a surface launch. All of their anti-ship missiles were fired from conventional tubes underwater, but the Soviet fleet had to use special external containers, which are much more complicated, more expensive, and less reliable.[21] The

---

[21] Admiral Berzin was wrong in his description of U.S. submarine missile capability. Five Regulus missile submarine used a deck launch system that required the submarine to fire their missiles on the surface. The USS *Tunny* (SSG 282) and the USS *Barbero* (SSG 317) were World War II fleet boats modified to carry Regulus. They were joined in 1958 by two submarines designed and built for the purpose of carrying Regulus missiles, the USS *Grayback* (SSG 574), the USS *Growler* (SSG 577), and later by the nuclear powered USS *Halibut* (SSGN).

submarine continued to approach the aircraft carrier, coming to periscope depth every four hours for communication sessions to receive additional targeting information from the base.

Berzin analyzed the carrier's route. Most likely, he believed, the carrier was following a specific depth of water, to enable their U.S. submarine's long range sonar to detect K 184. It is possible that they had already found her because Berzin had operated all day at a speed of nineteen knots creating thunder in the ocean. He discussed the results of the missile attack with his Executive Officer. Could an aircraft carrier survive a missile attack? How accurate were the fleet headquarters coordinates? In directing the submarine to the aircraft carrier, the base used reports from reconnaissance surface ships, another submarine, aircraft, satellites, and the coastal reconnaissance fleet. The reports from these assets were immediately sent to the fleet headquarters where a special staff office plotted the information. The information was averaged, analyzed, and only then passed on to the submarine. The result was that Berzin should be able to launch a missile strike on the aircraft carrier at a very great range. Throughout all stages of the process many people were involved and although some errors could be prevented, the technique used was not perfect. Transmission of updated information must be done quickly or it becomes obsolete, and the missile might not reach its target. It is the responsibility of the submarine's Commanding Officer in peacetime to give them a just tribute, but in wartime it may be dismissed.

At the next communications session, Berzin inspected the horizon with the help of radar and immediately saw his goal on the radar screen. It turned out that it was the aircraft carrier thirty miles distant. The commander decided to close to make sonar contact with them and to conduct a training torpedo attack. The submarine dove and began an approach on the aircraft carrier. According to his calculations sonar would hear the carrier in about two hours. At 12:10 p.m. the Commanding Officer slowed the submarine to six knots, a few minutes later sonar heard the noise of the carrier's screws. He then announced on the submarine's broadcast system, "This is a Drill, Battle Stations, we will conduct a simulated torpedo attack on a U.S. aircraft carrier." The crew took their stations for a torpedo attack and began to determine course and speed of the aircraft carrier and the distance to it. A few minutes later the necessary parameters were automatically entered into the torpedo. Finally, Berzin commanded: "Make ready the torpedo!" From the torpedo compartment he received the report, "Ready the torpedo – done!" He then gave the last command, "torpedo fire!" If it was wartime, the torpedo really would have come out of the submarine's torpedo tube and move rapidly toward the aircraft carrier. The simulated attack ended, and the submarine began to move away from the aircraft carrier to contact their base from a safe distance.

Berzin, having already been awake for two days, closed his eyes in the control room for about thirty minutes only to be awakened by a missive from the Chief of Staff of the Soviet Navy which read, "Indirectly, I assume that you are being followed by carrier strike group escorts. Report how many surface ships, aircraft, and active sonar you have observed in the sector." Berzin read the radio message and laughed because the text matched the thoughts that had haunted him for two days. When he closed to detect the aircraft carrier he might have been identified by her surface escorts using their sonars in the active mode. The sounds of sonar echo ranging were heard almost continuously for the past twelve hours. The impression was that U.S. forces had discovered or were about to discover the submarine. K 184 came to periscope depth for a communications session in the afternoon, the commander saw through the periscope; calm sea, cloudless sky and no one was there. He had full visibility to the horizon and sighted not a single ship, but at the same time he heard in the background sonar signals, a clear indication of the presence of the aircraft carriers escorts. From this he felt ill at ease. He said; "The ships are near! But my eyes have seen an absolutely clear ocean and sky." On several levels, Berzin understood that the submarine probably had not been detected. Now it was necessary to respond to the Chief of Staff of the Navy's radio transmission. Any transmission by radio from a submarine violates its security because it can be used to determine their location. At the fleet headquarters no one thought about that, they needed to immediately satisfy their curiosity.

———

Patrols normally lasted fifty days, perhaps longer. If there is no contact with foreign ships, submarines, and anti-submarine aircraft or there are no emergencies, the days are just one like the other. According to statistics there are two or three emergency situations per patrol. These can include fire, loss of electrical power, seawater leak, anything related to radiation safety, damage to equipment and weapons, and issues related to management of the submarine. An emergency is when the crew cannot rapidly eliminate all of the consequences. Each crew member's daily watch cycle includes eight hours on duty, eight hours asleep. The other eight hours are occupied by breakfast, lunch, dinner, evening tea, participation in general ship events, and finally personal affairs. Once a week sailors, midshipmen, and the officers are required to attend political training, such as Marxist Leninist studies.

Officers lived in two and four person cabins and the sailors and midshipmen lived in ten man bunkrooms. Nowhere can a man be alone. Often it turns out that the men living in adjacent beds have completely incompatible personalities. Submariners on a patrol were forced to lead a sedentary lifestyle, sleeping in a space only twenty to thirty meters from their military watch post. There was no Sun, no fresh air, no women, and they were separated from their families. If a surface ship is on a long trip, the crew at least sees their surroundings. On a submarine no one sees anything – even the route chart can only be seen by a few of the crew, for others it is forbidden. The route and operating area of the submarine are confidential information. For over fifty days, the men have no idea where they are.

To alleviate some of the issues, Berzin went to his Deputy for Political Affairs and told him that he had talked to Hitrenko about making space for a smoking room and an additional shower compartment in the secondary spaces. A smoking room had not been provided in this class of submarine. Hitrenko agreed with this plan and a smoking room was established. The temperature in the smoking room was somewhere around forty degrees Celsius (102 degrees Fahrenheit). A wet sheet was hung and it was rapidly saturated with nicotine. The pleasure of smoking in these conditions was questionable. The Political Officer said bluntly, "The smell is terrible!" When two people start smoking a minute later they are immersed in a gray fog, but despite this, the smoking room almost always had a line.

For the shower, no more than one or two people could use the existing shower at the same time. The fan pulls air out of the shower, passes it through a filter and then back into the shower in a closed cycle. The new shower room was a great improvement.

Almost every evening after tea Hitrenko spoke to Berzin. One evening, they spoke of an event that happened in the Baltic Fleet at Riga in 1970. A surface ship under the leadership of a Deputy for Political Affairs, Captain Third Rank Sablin, led a crew rebellion and arrested the Commanding Officer. The ship passed into the Gulf of Riga; at the exit of the strait they were stopped by fleet aviation units, which began dropping warning bombs. This influenced some of the participants in the uprising. One of them freed the Commanding Officer who quickly went up to the bridge. With a pistol he wounded Sablin and restored order. The ship returned to base.

The crew was disbanded, part of them suffered administrative punishment and the other part was convicted and sentenced with Sablin to capital punishment.[22] At trial, Sablin said that he was not going to take the ship to any foreign country, but was going to Leningrad, where he would request to make a statement on the radio about his disagreement with the policies of the current regime. Berzin was struck by this story. And when he was alone, he continued to think about Sablin. Suddenly he remembered Lieutenant Schmidt a hero of the 1905 revolution who had led a mutiny in Sevastopol on the cruiser *Ochakov*. He was arrested, tried, and executed.[23] He began to compare their lives and came to one conclusion; both had violated their oath of office which he regarded at all times as the foundation of the military

---

[22] The Mutiny of the frigate *Sterozhevoy* (Sentry) was a great embarrassment to the Soviet Navy. The event was hushed up and all documentation about the mutiny and subsequent trails were classified. A well-documented account of the event was recently published in *The Last Sentry* a book by Gregory Young and Nate Braden.
[23] On November 26, 1905 a mutiny started on board the *Ochakov* and all of its officers were chased away from the ship. The rebels invited Schmidt to take the command of the ship and to lead the revolutionary squadron. In ninety minutes they were defeated by government ships led by the battleship *Rostislav*.

and the people. These men had sworn to be faithful to their country, their people, and their government or king. Without this commitment the military cannot exist. If a person, for whatever reason, cannot fulfill his oath, he should leave the military to continue to act on his own convictions. In both cases many innocent people were lost or suffered. Today in print and on television there is a debate on the rehabilitation of Sablin, and talk about him being a fighter against stagnation. In Berzin's point of view, Schmidt and Sablin deliberately violated their oath of office and therefore cannot be used as good examples for Navy personnel. Imagine that if today some nuclear powered submarine with nuclear ballistic missiles went to sea without permission and its commander announces on the radio that he disagrees with the current regime's policies. What impression would that give to the whole world? No one would need to cut the branch on which they sat.

Aware of their newest orders, Berzin went into the chart room. The Navigator reported, "We will reach patrol area number two — their destination — in two hours." The Chief Medical Officer, Major Ushakov, reported to him that Midshipman Ponomarev had an appendicitis attack. He had decided to operate with the help of a Midshipman chemist, who before this trip had worked as a nurse in a hospital surgical ward. Ushakov said that such operations are common on patrols, but on this class of submarines it was not routine. The Doctor had his own cabin, which was also the outpatient facility. The operation was going to be conducted on the wardroom table in the officers' mess. The mess was washed with soap including the floor, walls, and desks, and when the doctor and the chemist were ready the Commanding Officer announced on the ships broadcasting system the forthcoming operation. He cautioned the crew that there was to be no interruption, maintaining a stable angle, depth and speed were necessary for the safety of their shipmate. The operation began and many of the crew feared for their comrade. Finally, the Doctor came to the officer's mess doorway and reported, "The operation is complete and the patient feels well." Ponomarev was then moved into the Doctor's cabin.

The submarine arrived at the assigned patrol area number two and started to look for U.S. surface ships. In the latest radio communications session, fleet headquarters had ordered the submarine to resume conducting the communications session every eight hours instead of every four hours. It was very useful because Berzin was extremely tired and with this schedule he could catch up on some of his sleep. At 6:00 p.m. the emergency alarm was heard which immediately pulled the commander from his makeshift bed in the control room. The Executive Officer reported to him, "There is a fire in the 7th compartment!" Then came the reports, "The air filter caught fire and the fire has been extinguished. There is negligible smoke in the space." Berzin and the Engineer Officer immediately began to give commands to the fire suppression team. Hitrenko came to the control room and received a report on the situation. He did not intervene and sat silently not far from the Commanding Officer. After about five minutes the compartment reported that "The fire was extinguished." Berzin ordered the air in the compartment analyzed and to report the causes of the filter fire. Ten minutes later, the petty officer in charge of the 7th compartment reported that the carbon monoxide level was three times normal. The cause of the fire was a mistake made by the sailor involving the regulation of the filter. Measures were taken to restore the compartment to its normal composition of air. Berzin then ordered the Engineer Officer to conduct an investigation of this case and the Executive Officer to do a staff analysis of the emergency. A fire on a submarine is a terrible and very dangerous event. That day, the casualty was minor and over quickly. The crew escaped with little fear and the submarine sustained almost no damage. In other cases it might have resulted in a more serious accident and even disaster, as it happened with the submarine *Komsomolets*. [24]

From the very beginning of the patrol, Hitrenko had been worried that a submarine of the U.S. *Sturgeon* class was following them. This is a very serious enemy. The most important advantage of the *Sturgeon* class was that it was several times quieter than K 184 and their sonar system was much better. The *Sturgeon* class could hear from a much

---

[24] Admiral Berzin refers to the loss of K 278, *Komsomolets* in April 1989, which sank in the Norwegian Sea following a fire in the 7th compartment. The Commanding Officer and forty one members of the crew were lost. The K 278 was honored by becoming one of the few Soviet submarines to be given an actual name.

greater distance than the Soviet submarines. For example, they could hear the Echo II at a distance of fifty miles, whereas, the Soviet submarines could detect the American only within a distance of five miles. This gave the American's opportunity to secretly follow the Soviets, identify their tactics, and with the outbreak of hostilities they would be the first to use a weapon. In the early years of the construction of nuclear submarines the U.S. did not have such an advantage. When earlier U.S. nuclear submarines tried to follow at short range, they put themselves and their adversary at risk of collision. Once a U.S. submarine collided underwater with the stern of a Soviet submarine and bent the propulsion line shaft. All these cases caused Soviet submariners to think about how to avoid such collisions when they were being covertly tracked. Soviet science and industry could not overtake the U.S. in these matters, so the commanding officers of nuclear submarines had to be content with compensating for lagging development by using appropriate tactics. While on a patrol the commanding officers of submarines are always aware of this problem and each in his own way tried to resolve this issue.

A submarine is a really quiet object. Quite often they are only discovered at a very close range. Using stealth, a submarine can close another ship remaining undetected while determining their course, speed, and range. Sounds in seawater are distributed by very complex laws, in some cases submarines can be heard by sonar at great distances, and in other cases only very short distances. Hearing very little, they still have to determine who owns the noise, whether it is a submarine, surface ship, vessel, fishing seiners, marine animals, or any of many natural sounds of the sea. Sonarmen try to identify a contact with their ears, and this, of course, does not always work, but such are the demands on them. On the shore and at sea they are systematically trained by listening to recordings of standard noises of submarines, surface ships, and other objects. With the discovery of any noise in the sea, sonar records it on tape to compare it with other reference noises. If the noise is the same as a standard recorded noise, then they can immediately tell what object they have detected. The well qualified sonarmen can determine what kind of noise they are hearing, without listening to the reference tapes. All of this is quite difficult and depends on the individual.

Berzin did not know yet that the American submarines went into these issues much further. They had developed a specialized computer, which analyzes the frequency, harmonics, the power of sound, and then compares it to the reference entries to provide a classification. In addition there were special devices, which mimic different sounds made by a surface ship, fishing seiner, pods of dolphins, and other sounds that allowed American submarine commanding officers to conceal their actions and to confuse our ships and submarines.

That evening, the Mate, Chertkov, approached Berzin saying, "Comrade Commander, I've brought you horse feathers, do you want to take a look?" Smiling, Berzin took the Captain's logbook and the plan of the day for the next day and approved them. Then they discussed the upcoming crew holiday on their return from this patrol. After discussing the main issues Berzin asked: "Alexander where will you go on vacation?"

Chertkov thought and slowly replied, "I'm a bachelor. I have many women friends in Moscow, Sevastopol, and Riga. I will visit some of them during the holiday. I will be alone, free as a bird."

Berzin loved his family and when left alone, the loneliness gnawed at him like a hungry wolf. He did not understand how one could live for thirty-five years and still not be married. So he asked Chertkov, "Do you ever have a feeling of loneliness?" Chertkov immediately replied, "I saw how my family and special friends lived and I do not envy them." Berzin knew a little about his life and it had not been the easiest. Chertkov was born in Lviv.[25] His father and older brother constantly drank and died early, it had happened before his eyes. Even then he swore to himself that he would never touch liquor. He graduated college with great difficulty, but in the Navy service he was no worse than many others. There was talk of him as a candidate for

---

[25] The city, Lviv, was a major Polish and Jewish cultural center in the Ukraine until the outbreak of World War II. The historical heart of Lviv with its old buildings and cobblestone roads survive World War II and the ensuing Soviet presence largely unscathed.

command. Wherever he went, many wondered why he did not drink. On occasions in times of slow promotion, officers often gathered where vodka was flowing like a river, and made toasts, drinking the glass to the bottom. Many pestered him and tried to force him to drink, but it did not work.

After tea that evening, Hitrenko spoke with Berzin about his own life and service. Berzin had told him that he had just read a book about Tukhachevsky, Yakir, and Uborevich.[26] From the book the conversation turned to their arrests in 1937. Hitrenko suddenly said, "In fact, in 1937, I was also living in a prison camp." Berzin, surprised, asked "What? Hitrenko you were then only a child." "Yes. When I was twelve years old my father and mother were arrested three days after a party where my tipsy father unwisely told a political anecdote. They were tried, each given ten years. They were sent to different camps, where they later died. I was arrested a week later. The rules of the camp required children to accompany their adults. There I stayed for about a year. By some miracle my cousins rescued me from the camp. I will remember the year of 1937 for the rest of my life. It is not possible to describe it, the constant feeling of hunger and cold, humiliation, and endless work." Hitrenko paused and then continued, "In general, under Stalin there was order, strict discipline, but not now." Hitrenko finished on a positive note, "Okay, Commander! Let's go to sleep. Tomorrow in Moscow the 24th Congress of the Communist Party will be reporting their results. Do not forget to hold a meeting on this special occasion."

The last few days Berzin had not felt well. He had a headache, weakness, and was indifferent to everything. From a conversation with the doctor, he realized that many of the crew were also in such a state. In the morning he was awakened by the Navigator who reported, "Comrade Commander, in five minutes we will reach the mark you

---

[26] Marshal Mikhail Tukhachevsky and other senior military officers including Iona Yakir and Leronim Uborevich were accused of anti-Soviet conspiracy and sentenced to death. They were executed on the night of June 11–12 1937, immediately after the verdict was delivered by a Special Session of the Supreme Court of the Soviet USSR. The arrests and trial had been ordered by Stalin who had actually concocted a fictitious plot to get rid of his most famous and important Soviet generals in a believable manner.

made on the chart." The submarine rocked. Berzin looked at the in-clinometer, the arrow indicated a five degrees roll, and then his eyes fell on the depth gauge. The depth was eighty meters. The appearance of roll at that depth meant that on the surface there was a storm. It became clear to him that the ascent to periscope depth needed to be canceled. In such circumstances the astrological navigation system could not be used.

The storm not only canceled the planned ascent, but it created troubling issues with the latrine. The most painful activity on the submarine was to visit the toilet space. Berzin had long dreamed of meeting the designer and taking retribution. The size of the space re-sembled a coffin. Above the toilet hung a massive fan that many people forgot about until they smashed their forehead into it. On the left and right were sets of valves and on the door right in front of the bulkhead were the "instructions for operating the toilet." If they were uninten-tionally violated, then the contents of the bowl could fly right back at you. Breaking the "rules" of the toilet would paint the compartment in warm brown tones with a distinctive smell. Even when performing all the rules, it could occur in individual cases. All these shortcomings are amplified many times when the submarine enters a storm and begins to roll even when submerged.

The submarine has its own characteristics, not only in the latrine, but also in other domestic issues like washing, doing the laundry, and throwing out garbage and food leftovers. Berzin remembered his ser-vice on diesel submarines. When they went on patrol, they completely filled the water tanks, save one cup. They washed with seawater using a special soap. The doctor regularly provided wipes soaked in alcohol to clean the body. On a nuclear submarine, however, there is an evap-oration plant, which distilled freshwater from seawater for use in the main power plant and for domestic purposes, such as drinking and bathing. On a patrol, the crew was allowed two showers every seven to ten days and was able to wash small things, but there was no laundry on the boat and there was nowhere to dry underwear and bed linens. Each crew member was issued pants, shirt and socks, two sheets and a pillowcase. Dirty clothes were collected and on return to port they were recycled. Underwear called "one-offs" was designed for single use.

Practically they could withstand quite a large number of washings. Outerwear consisted of dark blue jackets, trousers, and beret caps that were changed in the field no more than two times. On each jacket was a white cloth ribbon, where the officers wrote their positions, and the sailors and Midshipmen wrote their battle station. One of our boats on patrol went to Somalia and for a short time moored at a pier. One of these worn out jackets was thrown into the trash, but the officer forgot to rip out the tape. The black man, who served the pier, fished the jacket out of the trash, washed and was wearing it. On the tape was written, "The Commander of Battle Group Three." The People's Commissariat for Internal Affairs (NKVD) was horrified. The commander got a new jacket and tried to trade it for the one with the tape, but it was no deal because the old man valued the title on the piece. Each day the crew had fun watching the "Commander of Battle Group Three" sweeping the pier.

———

Berzin had long been aware of a personnel policy in the Navy that ensured the submarines did not include persons of "non-indigenous nationalities" such as; Jews, Germans, Poles, Koreans, and those who served Yeshe.[27] Under any pretext they could be removed. On the other hand officers and warrant officers of indigenous nationalities who were constantly drinking and were frequently shirking their responsibilities in submarines for years could not be removed. Although their commanders requested almost on their knees the answer was always the same, "Educate!" These officers constituted the fertile ground on which flourished many accidents and caused the death of many people.

Summoned to the control room by the Deputy for Political Affairs, Zubkov, Berzin discussed all the details of the rally for the 24th Congress of the Communist Party. The crew was to remain in their spaces — except those that were assigned to the control room — during the time

---

[27] Yeshe was the founder-figure of the Nyingma tradition of Tibetan Buddhism. Buddhists suffered more than any other religious community in the Soviet Union with many being expelled and accused of being "Japanese spies" and "the people's enemies."

the ceremony of the 24th Congress address was to be played on the ship's broadcast system. Everything went calmly and uneventfully. They were all used to the Congress and expected nothing special would come to their lives. On the surface, the storm was already in the third day of shaking the submarine, even at a depth of eighty meters. Everybody wanted to go home, but time was running very slowly.

The Commanding Officer knew from his experience on other submarines patrols that the closer to the end of the patrol, there were more cases of sleeping on duty, negligence in the maintenance of equipment, and disregard of safety procedures. He had discussed this concern with his officers who decided to take measures to reduce these types of behavior. At the next communications session he received the following,

> "To the Commanding Officer from the Fleet Commander -- by 8:00 p.m. on April 16 you are to take station in area number five. Your objective is to find a group of U.S. military transports. Conduct a training attack with missile and torpedo weapons."

After plotting the coordinates — and with much discussion between Berzin and Hitrenko — it became evident that despite the brevity of the order, the submarine could currently deliver a missile strike on the group of transports because of the range.

At night, the submarine again came to periscope depth to receive the communication session with the shore and received the following radio message.

> "To the Commanding Officer from the Fleet Commander — At 5:00 a.m. you will receive targeting from two airplanes — At 6:00 a.m. conduct a training missile strike on the group of transports."

Berzin read the message and started work on developing the next solution. The two aircraft were already in flight and had to come a great distance to find this group of ocean transports. Once they located them they had to determine the transports' latitude, longitude, course, speed, and pass it to the submarine. This work is called targeting. The pilots knew that in wartime that their air defense system would not allow fighter jets to destroy them in the initial section of their route. Today, they were met by American electronic warfare aircraft, which immediately began to harass them. At 4:50 a.m. we came to periscope depth to receive the targeting information. The radio operator reported contact with the aircraft. The pilots with great difficulty had determined the location of the transports. They were being continuously jammed which interfered with the operation of their airborne radar and radio traffic to us. The U.S. aircraft did their job conscientiously. Berzin saw on his radar screen a few marks of surface targets, but within a few seconds they were gone. The radio operator reported the plane had reported the latitude, longitude, course, and speed of the transports. When this targeting information had been received, we dove to a depth of eighty meters and began the pre-launch preparation of the missile system. The training rocket attack was successful.

In the regular communications session we received direction to move closer to the transport group in the shortest possible time to a distance where we could track them by sonar or visually through the periscope. Also a radio message was received,

> "To the Commanding Officer from the Fleet Commander – At 4:00 p.m. conduct a second training missile strike on the group of transports targeting them by your own means of observation."

After the first missile attack the Commanding Officer had not received any more information about the group. Berzin and the Navigator finished the calculations; it was not a very rosy picture. To get close enough to the submarine transports they needed to increase the speed to twenty knots for about eight hours. Of course the submarine would give up the element of surprise because at that speed they would be very noisy, but what the fleet commander ordered must be performed. In addition, finding this group in the open ocean would be extremely difficult, like finding a needle in a haystack. Berzin gave the necessary commands to begin the process of intercepting the transports. Twice the submarine came up for a communication session, but the fleet staff provided no new information. At 3:00 p.m. the submarine slowed to six knots to listen to the horizon on sonar. Five minutes later sonar reported, "The horizon is clear." Berzin understood that the probability of intercepting the group of transports was very small. The Navigator charted the probable location of the transports. It was an elongated patch of ocean one hundred eight miles long and thirty-two miles wide. Berzin looked at it and, turning to the Navigator, said, "It looks like a sausage, but we will not choke on it." The submarine ascended to periscope depth and Berzin inspected the horizon through the periscope and radar. No contacts were found. They then submerged and continued the search for the transports on the intercept course. In the control room Hitrenko arrived, examined the situation and demanded that the Commanding Officer report on the scheduled upcoming second missile attack. Berzin made his report: "Missile attack was not executed because the group of transports was not found."

Hitrenko, slyly smiling, interrupted him, "Commanding Officer of the *Kalashnikov* was dismissed because he was late conducting a missile attack."

Berzin continued to report, "We do not know the site of the specific group of transports. It is impossible to shoot at a likely place."

Hitrenko advised, "Take the average bearing, the average distance from the chart and shoot."

Berzin at once replied, "No, I will not shoot this sausage using up good missiles in vain."

Hitrenko replied, "What sausage? Choose any expression and I do not insist on the missile-attack, but keep in mind that I told you about the *Kalashnikov*."

The submarine surfaced to periscope depth for radio transmission to the Navy headquarters. Berzin reported that the group of transports was not detected by the submarine's means.

At the same time, radio received from the fleet headquarters.

"To the Commanding Officer from the Fleet Commander – Start moving toward your base."

Finally they were going home. This order was communicated to all of the compartments. The crew began to talk with joy. They were already tired of the cruise and wanted to be home with their relatives and friends.

During the patrol, several members of the crew had grown luxurious beards and mustaches; and many of them now shaved in order to not frighten their loved ones. Berzin hardly slept that night, thinking about the upcoming meeting with his wife and children. Finally, the Navigator announced, "Only five miles to point number ten" — their rendezvous point.

The Commanding Officer and his crew began to prepare for the last surfacing of this patrol. The submarine came to periscope depth and Berzin surveyed the horizon through the periscope. It was still dark, and straight ahead he saw the white masthead light of the escort ship *Penguin*. The submarine surfaced. Berzin went up the vertical ladder to the upper conning tower hatch, which had not been opened during the entire patrol. On the bridge, dawn had not yet arrived and there was an overcoming smell of fish and seaweed. The smallest microorganisms stuck to the whole body of the submarine and in the darkness radiated a mysterious shimmer. Four miles before joining the escort ship the radio operator reported, "We have established radio contact with the *Penguin*."

The submarine continued to move into the base ahead of the escort ship. Daylight revealed that almost all of the crew was pale, some now looked more yellow, or even blue. The submarine entered the harbor and moored alongside a pier. On the pier, submariners, representatives of the staff, and an orchestra were assembled. Hitrenko descended from the submarine on the gangway to the pier. Then his Operations Officer, Vetkin, announced loudly, "Comrade Rear Admiral, the personnel of the squadron are assembled on this occasion to honor the submarine's return from patrol." Hitrenko greeted the crews of the other submarines. During this time, Berzin assembled his crew on the deck of his submarine. On the pier, Hitrenko approached the Chief Political Officer, Captain Volgin; they embraced. After that, Hitrenko, Volgin, and Vetkin climbed the ladder back on to the submarine; Berzin gave the command, "Attention! Eyes left!" And he came forward to meet Hitrenko, who greeted the crew and congratulated them on the successful completion of the patrol and he assigned the crew's next task. They were to remain on combat duty on the base until May 5th. All of the faces darkened because while on duty, they would not be able to see their families.

On the morning of May 1, a ceremony was held on each submarine and they raised the naval flag. The holiday orders were read, most of the other crews were encouraged to take leave. Then he ordered his off watch crew to the barracks to rest. He remained on the boat with the duty watch.

The next day Berzin woke up early in the morning with severe chills and a sore throat. After breakfast he went to see his doctor, who measured his temperature at thirty-nine degrees Centigrade (102.9 *degrees* Fahrenheit), gave him some tablets, and offered to have him go to the infirmary. He refused because that evening the submarine was going to move to the ammunition pier to offload the missiles that had passed their storage time limit. The Head of Operations, Captain Vetkin, arrived to accompany Berzin to the unloading pier. The Doctor had told Vetkin about the state of the Commanding Officer's health, but he did not react to it. Berzin barely got to the bridge with the effects of his dizziness, chills, and nausea; but his pride and sense of responsibility pushed him to accomplish the task. No one was going to command his submarine and replace him.

The next day began with a meeting of submarine commanding officers and political officers with the Chief of Staff, Captain First Rank Alexandrov. In a somber voice, he began to address the assembly, "Comrades, we will be visited by the Commander in Chief on Saturday. The purpose of his travel is not known. All military training is to stop. Instead we must each inspect our territory, and clean up the barracks and submarines. Pay special attention to uniforms, putting them in perfect condition. Fleet Commander Glebov will personally check the dress code in conjunction with comrade Commander Romasheva.

Additionally, he ordered the submarine commanding officers to inspect the condition of their crew and to leave in ranks only those whose uniforms met statutory requirements. Then he directed Commander Romasheva to make the same inspection of the squadron staff and the compound; only then would he check himself. The same meeting was repeated the next day.

"The Navy requires you to toughen your standards for your crews, to strengthen your supervision to those guilty of misconduct, and to apply severe sanctions." Berzin was sitting and listening to all these depressing words. Alexandrov continued, "Tomorrow we will assemble on the parade ground. At 8:00 a.m. the commanding officers of the submarines will check dress the code of their crews, and at 10:00 a.m. Rear Admiral Hitrenko will do the same." By the afternoon the meeting was over and they all went into the dining room. After that Berzin assembled his officers and told them about the meeting. Before dinner his crew brushed their uniforms, washed, shaved, and prepared for the inspection.

Friday at 8:00 a.m. the squadron personnel assembled on the parade ground and the commanders of submarines began to inspect the uniforms of their crew. The Squadron Duty Officer, however, gave the command, "The commanding officers of submarines are to report to the headquarters of Rear Admiral Hitrenko."

The commanding officers went to the headquarters, and staff continued to stand on the parade ground. Chief of Staff, Alexandrov, waited twenty minutes and then approached the assembly. He was playing the part of the Commander in Chief, and all submarine senior officers greeted him, "Good morning, Comrade Admiral of the Fleet" and after each greeting he gave an assessment: "Two points, three points...." After a half an hour the squadron, with difficulty, obtained an estimate of five points. The whole effect was spoiled by a flock of chickens that popped up onto the field. Then the squadron marched past the podium several times where Chief of Staff Alexander stood portraying the Commander In Chief. Here it was necessary to show good alignment, solid steps, and simultaneous turning of heads when "Eyes Right" was ordered.

Hitrenko went to the commanding officers and immediately began to instruct them by saying, "The Commander of the Navy inspected the Sergeyev squadron yesterday. Two officers were nearly dismissed for the poor condition of their crew's uniforms. He told them that they were unqualified for their position. Be ready to report on the status of military training on your submarines, on their technical condition, and other matters." After lunch Berzin checked that the dress code of the crew complied with the regulations; only three officers and three sailors did not meet the requirements. There were a lot of reasons. Berzin had served in the Navy for twenty years and for as many years there had been a problem with uniforms.

Design of uniforms came from the heads of the various services. More or less they were fit for service in Moscow, but for service on ships and submarines, they were not practical, because the uniforms were not made to be used while working with equipment. Service in the north or in Kamchatka and in the Black Sea is quite different. Especially there were problems with shoes. In the north and in Kamchatka the shoes had to work in deep snow drifts, and in the warm south, the same shoes made your legs feel like they were in a sauna. In this little naval town there was only one tailor shop, and the time to fit new uniforms took several months or even years. The base had no shops to fit uniforms for the young sailors, who were continuing to grow in size. Special clothing for nuclear submarines was always in chronically short supply — it was quickly worn out and torn. Crews in the submarine force resembled professional beggars who spend their days in the trash. In the evening, Hitrenko, for the second time that day, instructed the commanding officers: "Keep in mind that the Commander in Chief carries with him all kinds of uniforms. To coordinate the staff, he has a special man with the rank of Colonel. The Commander in Chief never announces in what uniform we should meet him." In the morning we will look at the way he is dressed, and then we will all change to that uniform. I've also made an arrangement with the fleet staff to tell us what uniform he will be wearing. So all of you, your officers and warrant officers remain in the barracks ready to change into your parade dress, casual jacket, or coat." Hitrenko paused and then continued, "Bukrimov your pigs and chickens from your part time farm roam all over. Catch all of them and do not release them. I particularly do not want to see any of them near the staff building and the hotel."

After this, he again ordered us to make everything tidy in barracks and in the territory. The Head of the Radiation Safety Service was instructed to clean up the road from the monument to the headquarters using soap and to cut the grass along the road. Where the grass has turned yellow, it was to be painted green. Again Saturday, as before at 8:00 a.m., the staff assembled on the parade ground. An hour later, all the Commanding officers were addressed by Hitrenko. He began, "The Commander in Chief directed us to be prepared for the meeting at 11:00 a.m. The commanding officers are to remain in the barracks. The staff is to be sent to the boat. The crews are to walk on their territory to remove all cigarette butts." Everyone went to their places. At 10:00 a.m. the Duty Officer called all commanding officers and gave orders for them to immediately report to Hitrenko. Again, the commanding officers went to headquarters, where Hitrenko gave the last order of the day, "Go to your boats and stay there; dress in casual jacket."

Berzin went to his boat and ordered the periscope raised so he could watch everything that was happening. He immediately turned the optics to high power, to see the Commander in Chief when he arrived. From the Kontrolno gate to the headquarters there were patrols of sailors with red flags to direct the approaching cars. Suddenly everyone began to move and run and then they froze. There was a long line of cars and for some reason they did not go to the headquarters. They drove toward the armory under construction and then to the property beyond. Out came a car from the headquarters heading for the construction site. The Fleet Command, Squadron, and Staff officers finally caught up with the Commander in Chief's car. They stayed there for about an hour, after which the cortege headed to the headquarters, where they again stopped, but the Commander in Chief did not go into the headquarters or the hotel, which was in front of headquarters. Berzin looked at his watch; it was time for lunch, and thought, "It is clear to me how this visit will be finished." There would be no parade or inspection.

He knew that the hotel had prepared a special lunch for the Commander in Chief and his entourage. Yesterday they had ordered the slaughter of two of Bukrimov's piglets for the guest. Two officers from the headquarters, Udaltsov and Serebrinkin, in diving suits and scuba gear spent hours fishing in the bay for scallops and sea cucumbers to use as a special delicacy. Hitrenko really knew how to entertain the Chiefs. While the Commander in Chief was having lunch, the Staff Officers of the fleet were having a quick lunch in the submariner's canteen, but they were not served the special dishes provided in the hotel. Although it was lunchtime, the crews of submarines were banned from the dining room. Finally, the Commander in Chief left the hotel and saw a huge boar passing the hotel followed by three fat pigs and finally the procession was completed by a pig-boy. Some wit had red leaded them with the following signs: Squadron Commander, Chief of the Political Department, Division Commander, and Chief of Staff. The Commander in Chief turned to Hitrenko and said: "Hitrenko, you have again shown fantastic disgust." After that, he smiled, got into his car and departed for the Nadvodnikam base. Crews were ordered to go to the cafeteria. After lunch Hitrenko told Berzin that tomorrow he considered himself on vacation.

The patrol had finally come to an end and Berzin was free to take leave and visit his family, but his responsibility for K 184 and his crew would continue until he was relieved of command in 1974. Coming home always welcomed submariners with surprises. Life went on.

MINTON'S EARLY COMMAND YEARS

I took command of USS *Guardfish* (SSN 612) in November 1970 during her long and challenging overhaul in Pascagoula, Mississippi.

The *Guardfish* was a *Thresher* class nuclear attack submarine. The class was renamed the *Permit* class after the tragic loss of the USS *Thresher* (SSN 593) on 10 April 1963. The *Guardfish* combined the endurance and environmental independence of nuclear power and deep submergence. She was driven by a single propeller and her advanced hydrodynamic hull provided optimum maneuverability and speed. Designed specifically for anti-submarine warfare missions, *Guardfish* was well suited to its difficult task.

During post-overhaul sea trials, we conducted underway tests on all of our equipment including a deep dive to test depth. On this trial, we were escorted by a diesel submarine to provide underwater telephone communications if there was any problem while we were submerged. Following completion of all tests, we surfaced and the diesel submarine was released to return to Key West, Florida. It took off at high speed on the surface and was soon out of sight over the horizon.

It wasn't much longer, however, before we discovered that all our high frequency antennas were shorted out and we were unable to send a critical message reporting that the sea trial was complete and that we were safely on the surface. Time was running out and soon the Commander Submarine Force Atlantic Fleet would initiate a Sub-Missing Report and all sorts of rescue forces would be activated. What to do? I had the searchlight brought to the bridge and we started signaling our diesel submarine escort by flashing on the low lying clouds. Much to my relief they saw the signal and reversed course and were able to send the important message for us. Sea trials are a very tense and difficult time for submarine families. In Pascagoula despite my assurances of a safe sea trial, everyone still remembered the loss of the USS *Thresher* (SSN 594) on their post-overhaul sea trials.

After leaving the shipyard in 1971, *Guardfish* transited from Cape Kennedy to Roosevelt Roads, Puerto Rico, where I had an experience that could have been career or life ending. We were headed south in the submarine transit lane into the Gulf Stream toward the city of San Juan. The transit lane is in relatively deep water approaching San Juan on the northern shore of Puerto Rico. I woke up in the wee hours of the morning with a feeling of apprehension for no apparent reason and I went up to the control room to take a look around. I checked the navigation chart and the position as given by the inertial navigation system (SINS), but I still was not reassured. Then I ordered the Officer of the Deck to slow, clear baffles, and come to periscope depth. Almost immediately the Navigator appeared in the control room telling me it was too soon we had more than an hour to go to reach the planned surfacing point. As I raised the periscope I sighted the city lights of San Juan covering about 130 degrees of the horizon before me. Realizing how close we had come to crashing into the island, I was in shock. I do not know what made me so restless that I woke up and decided to check our position. Perhaps the hull took on a different vibration as we approached shallower water. I just don't know.

Since that experience I have told this story to many officers at the Prospective Commanding Officer (PCO) School. My advice has always been that if you are uncomfortable with any situation react to it. Remember that you have much more experience than any of your officers. Do not hesitate to take action even if you cannot explain the reasons for doing so at that time.

After transiting the Panama Canal to the Pacific Ocean, we conducted sound trials in Carr Inlet near Seattle, Washington. During the trials we were submerged, suspended by chains from two large mooring buoys. Additionally, cables supplying the submarine with electric power were run through a replacement watertight hatch. This enabled us to shut down the reactor and individually record machinery noises. This wasn't my first experience with submerging suspended from those mooring buoys. In 1959 I was a junior officer on USS *Gudgeon* (SS 567) when we conducted sound trials in Carr Inlet. I had learned from that experience and we did not test the disconnect links.

Just after submerging (hanging from the buoys) while I was still in the control room, the telephone from the surface rang. Much to my surprise it was Admiral Rickover. The Admiral did not have much to say to me, but it was what he didn't say that was important. He was telling me, not so subtly, that he could find me no matter where *Guardfish* was located. This was another good example of his version of humor.

After the static phase hanging from the buoys there was an underway phase which required us to maneuver the submarine in a big race track while submerged. The objective of this was for us to pass close to an anchored hydrophone while they measured our radiated noise. The hydrophone also had a sound beacon for us to line up on. The beacon was supposed to be turned off when we had made the final turn for a pass, but it often was turned off early, leaving us without a reference point. The trial was running late causing the trial director to request that we conduct multiple runs without coming to periscope depth for a visual fix. The inlet was fair sized, but navigation was hazardous due to the large tides and currents in Puget Sound.

I foolishly agreed to this plan and after several passes we passed too close to the hydrophone and cut one of its mooring wires. The Officer of the Deck, Lieutenant Tim Guilfoil, was very upset and thought this might ruin his chances for promotion. I assured him that he had nothing to worry about. Happily, the only thing that resulted from this incident was that our screw was nicked where it had hit the mooring wire.

I had been dissatisfied with our screw's radiated noise ever since we left the shipyard in Pascagoula, Mississippi. Upon our return to Pearl Harbor, after leaving Carr Inlet, the screw was replaced with one with a much better sound signature. Nothing more was said about this incident and so it turned out to be a plus.

During our work up for deployment to the Western Pacific, we frequently conducted independent training exercises in an operating area just south of Oahu, Hawaii. As we were returning to Pearl Harbor, the Weapons Officer, Lieutenant Dick Woodward, came to the control room and requested we conduct a deep dive to pressure test a recently repaired fitting on one of the torpedo tubes. The test was part of the formal Sub-Safe documentation required after each repair to systems that were exposed to sea pressure. As an alternative it was possible to hydrostatically pressurize the torpedo tube, but that entailed a lot of preparation. I directed Dick to set up for the test and the Officer of the Deck to increase our depth as required. The setup in the torpedo room was taking way too long and I was getting that uncomfortable feeling that I had experienced before. Much to the Weapons Officer's disappointment I canceled the test and ordered the submarine to periscope depth. The Navigator took a fix and found we were two miles closer to shallow water off of Barbers Point than we thought we were. Reacting to my feelings had once again had been the right thing to do.

In early 1972 we deployed to the Western Pacific on a special operation. One day I was following a Soviet November class submarine and became so intent on the trailing that I forgot to check our position on the chart. The quartermaster on watch, QM1 (SS) C.F. Williams pulled me away from the plotting table and almost dragged me the navigational table where he showed me that we were approaching water shallower than our current operating depth. I immediately changed depth to a safe depth and continued tracking the Soviet submarine. This sailor could well have saved my career. I owed a lot to him for his vigilance.

It turned out that petty officer Williams had a storied history. He served on the USS *Queenfish* (SSN 651) crew while they explored and surveyed the Arctic seas north of Russia and visited the North Pole, no small feat. He then served as a riverboat pilot in Vietnam where he received numerous combat awards. Shortly after he came aboard, I heard a rumor from the crew that our new quartermaster had the number twenty-eight tattooed on his arm which represented the number of North Vietnamese he had killed up close with a knife. This sounded a bit unbelievable so I had the Executive Officer bring me his service record. Yes, there were lots of commendations and bronze star medals. All the citations in his record did not include much detail, which is common in black operation awards. I concluded he might be the real thing.

Unknown to me, Williams had a habit of going ashore in marine fatigues instead of the required Navy uniform. One night in Guam he went over to the barracks of the small marine detachment which supported the Naval Station as security guards. Apparently there was a fight during which Williams took on and beat up four marines, putting one of them in the hospital. The shore patrol was called and brought Williams back to *Guardfish*. The Executive Officer wanted to take him to Captain's Mast to be disciplined. I told the Executive Officer to handle it himself. The next day a young Marine Major came to the submarine and asked to see me. The Major was dressed in his finest khakis and was razor sharp. The Executive Officer escorted him to my stateroom and left him to me. The Major explained that he wanted to let me know about the seriousness of the injuries sustained by his men and began listing the various injuries they had suffered. I interrupted him and said, "You're telling me that one sailor beat up four of your marines? I wouldn't have had balls enough to come and complain. I would be embarrassed to even show my face." With this he closed his notebook with a snap and asked permission to leave the ship. Although Williams frequently caused a problem when ashore, he was an exemplary sailor on board. The Executive Officer again came to me and asked what would Williams have to do for me to officially punish him? My answer was only if he were found messing around with the Commodore's daughter. I owed him that.

Over my years in submarines I had encountered a number of sailors like Williams who caused the majority of the submarine's disciplinary problems. While they gave the Executive Officer grief, I observed that most of them were very reliable at sea. If I was ever put in the position of boarding another ship at sea, they were the men I would want to accompany me. I was sure that if hostilities erupted they would be able to immediately react with deadly force, if necessary, and would not shoot me in the back in their excitement. These men are a disappearing breed of warriors.

During the previous routine upkeep in Guam the submarine tender made a modification to a valve in the reactor purification system. This modification was part of an authorized ship-alteration directed by the Bureau of Ships. It went easily and was not expected to be a problem. Unfortunately it did cause us some difficulty. During the special operation we began to receive low level readings of radioactivity in the reactor compartment. After monitoring this for some time we shut the plant down and made a reactor compartment entry. We found that one of the new welds made by the tender had developed a small pin-hole leak. We were unable to repair the weld without cooling the plant down and that was not possible at sea.

The Engineer Officer developed a plan to isolate the purification system and to lower its pressure through the primary sample sink. This scheme worked very well and stopped the leak. Isolating the purification system made us impose a restriction on the main coolant pump operation. I did not want to shift pumps from slow speed to fast speed as this would cause a Chalk River Unidentified Deposits (CRUD) burst resulting in increased long lived radioactivity material through the primary system. Under ordinary operation the purification system would clean up most of the CRUD before it plated out in the primary system's piping. If we continued to operate with main coolant pumps in slow speed we would avoid the adverse effects of a CRUD burst.

At the end of the special operation *Guardfish* had been scheduled to visit the U.S. Naval Base in Yokosuka, Japan. Because of the Japanese sensitivity to all things relating to radioactivity and my previous experience on board the USS *Swordfish* (SSN 579), I elected to inform my operational commander of our situation including my being limited to slow speed main coolant pumps. *Guardfish* was rerouted to Guam for repairs of this valve and a normal upkeep. The transit orders required us to make a speed of advance (SOA) of twenty knots and to remain undetected.

I don't know who planned this transit because it was extremely difficult to make that speed while conducting regular communications schedules without shifting the main coolant to high speed. When communicating submerged we were limited by our periscope to five or six knots. It must have been some non-nuclear trained officer! To make matters worse, the tender in Guam while trying to get ready for our arrival, requested us to send ahead all our work requests and lists of parts and consumables we needed. I, therefore, elected to communicate at night with *Guardfish* running broached, and running maximum speed available with our main coolant pumps remaining in slow speed. We were actually faster submerged, but by being broached at night we were able to meet the two requirements placed on us – twenty knot SOA and to still remain undetected.

During this refit in Guam I was assigned a second special operation and directed to depart as soon as possible.

The year was 1972 and the War in Vietnam was dragging on. Protests over the war reflected the growing dissatisfaction of the American public. Additionally our military was frustrated with the support the North Vietnamese were receiving by sea from their allies. Another submarine preparing for sea in Guam was sent ahead of *Guardfish* to the South China Sea to intimidate merchant ships supplying the North Vietnamese by broaching and showing their presence. *Guardfish* was reassigned to take their special operation in the Sea of Japan. Initially I was disappointed in this change of schedule and dreamed of being authorized to sink some of the merchants. After all our weapons practice no Cold War submarine had ever fired any weapon in anger.

As you will see it turned out that I drew the better straw and wound up conducting a historic trail of a Soviet Echo II submarine.

CHAPTER VI

Guardfish's Trail of K 184

This Chapter picks up where THE TRAIL page xxvi left off.

Submarine espionage, conducted throughout WWII, began in earnest with the advent of the nuclear submarine in 1954. For more than twenty years, "...the United States [had] sent thousands of men in cramped steel cylinders on spy missions off the rugged coasts of the Soviet Union. There, the job was to stay hidden, to gather information about the enemy's intentions and its abilities to wage war at sea. By their very nature, submarines were perfect for this task, designed to lurk nearly silent and unseen beneath the waves. They quickly became one of America's most crucial spy vehicles." [28] Unseen, yet always suspected, the possible presence of American submarine forces was a top threat to the USSR.

The main job of U.S. subs was to find, identify, and trail Soviet submarines, whether they were deploying from far flung Soviet bases, sitting outside our cities, or cruising the South China Sea. Their goal was to attempt to ascertain who they were, what they were, what their capabilities were, and where they were going. And they were to do so

---

[28] Sherry Sontag and Christopher Drew, with Annette Lawrence Drew, *Blind Man's Bluff ~ The Untold Story of American Submarine Espionage* (New York: Public Affairs, 1998), xii.

without being detected. Stealth and silence were our greatest assets. Unlike diesel subs, by the 1970s, those powered by a nuclear reactor could stay submerged for months at a time without having to recharge their batteries and replenish their air supply. Most importantly, they could run almost silently. The American nuclear navy – of which the U.S. submarine force was a significant component – was the brainchild of Admiral Hyman Rickover.

It has been said that Admiral Hyman Rickover had the most powerful impact on the U.S. Submarine force of any individual since John P. Holland, the inventor of the internal combustion, gasoline powered submarine. "Slight of physique, [Rickover] was an intellectual heavyweight with a strong will who influenced every aspect of the submarine community." [29] Known for being a philosopher, Rickover was to have said that, "One must learn to reach out, not to struggle for that which is just beyond, but to grasp at results which seem almost infinite." [30] In a statement that could easily be a Navy motto, he would also say, "To seek and accept responsibility, to persevere, to be committed to excellence, to be creative and courageous, to be unrelenting in the pursuit of intellectual development, to maintain high standards of ethics and morality, and to bring these basic principles of existence to bear through active participation in life – these are some of my ideas that must be met to achieve meaning and purpose in life." [31]

And so it was with the admonitions of Rickover echoing in my head, that I began what would be the trail of a lifetime.

---

[29] Naval Submarine League, *United States Submarines* (Hugh Lauter Levin Associates Inc., 2002), 169.
[30] Ibid 171.
[31] Hyman G. Rickover, *Thoughts on Man's Purpose in Life, Morgenthau Memorial Lecture*, 1982. Published in the Wall Street Journal, New York, September 15, 2015.

The chart below is *Guardfish's* overall 6,100 nautical mile track during the trail.

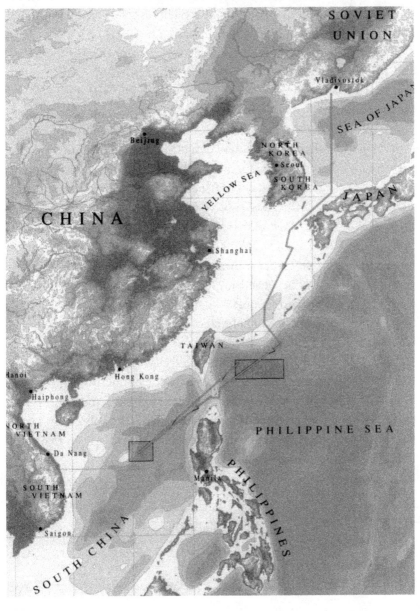

My operation orders did not direct me to follow him; the message had only instructed me to be alert for a deployment. Yet, as there was nothing else going on in the harbor — singularly strange — we followed the Echo II at high speed on a southern transit. We still had no way of knowing whether this was a sortie in response to the Haiphong bombings, but we were in pursuit.

During the next two days, the Soviet submarine frequently slowed and spent long periods at periscope depth. My estimate at the time was that he was probably receiving detailed orders from his Naval Commander.

While waiting for the Echo II, *Guardfish* was able to slow which significantly extended our sonar detection range and, much to our surprise and alarm, we were periodically able to detect at least two and possibly three other Soviet submarines in the area. I remember being slightly irritated with the Executive Officer, Lieutenant Commander Larry G. Vogt. It seemed that every time I turned the command duty over to him, sonar would detect another Soviet submarine. This made it hard for me to get any rest. At no time did we have all the contacts simultaneously and because they had similar almost identical sound characteristics we were unable to determine if we were dealing with three or four Soviet nuclear submarines.

The sonar signatures of all of our submarine contacts were classified as HENs. The acronym stands for HOTEL, ECHO, and NOVEMBER, the first generation class of Soviet nuclear submarines. They had identical reactor power plants, propulsion machinery, and therefore nearly identical sound characteristics. The submarines were moving slowly towards the Tsushima Straits, the southern exit from the Sea of Japan into the East China Sea.

Chartlet of Trail in the Sea of Japan

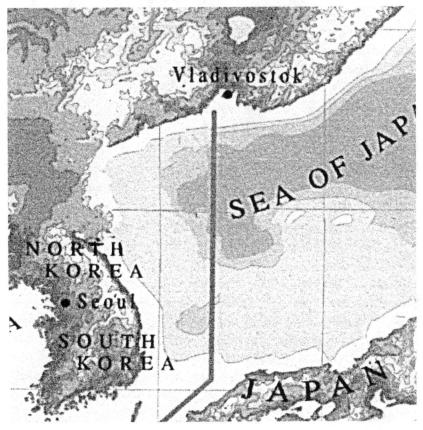

11 May.[32] *Depth one hundred meters, speed twelve and a half knots. K 184 turns off course 90 degrees every hour to listen astern to hear if any American submarines were trailing us. Life on board a submarine is organized and falls into a routine. From the intelligence summary:*

> *"There are six strike carriers and two helicopter carriers in Vietnamese waters."*

---

[32] In the following chapters italics are used to differentiate Admiral Berzin's entries from Captain Minton's.

During the broadcast, electronic support measures (ESM) detected a AN/APS-20 radar carried by a U.S. P-2 Neptune anti-submarine warfare (ASW) aircraft. The signal strength was weak. We changed course and dove to two hundred meters. Thirty minutes later, the Missile Officer, Captain Third Rank V.I. Tsimbalenko, came to the control room to report that there was a leak in the cable raceway in missile container six. It wasn't hermetically sealed and it contained a missile with a nuclear combat section. The missiles with nuclear combat sections were in containers one, two, five, and six. The missiles with the conventional explosive combat sections were in containers three, four, seven, and eight. If the container was flooded, that meant that the missile would have to be taken out of service, and was a potential weapons casualty. From the start of the deployment we were vexed by this situation. What to do in this case? Having heard the Missile Officer's report and suggestions from the Engineer Officer, Captain Second Rank M.S. Bayburin, I decided to open the drain valve in compartment seven so that the water in the cable raceway in container six would drain into the bilge so the leakage rate could be measured – ten liters a minute and periodically I ordered the water to be pumped from the bilge overboard. In addition, I decided to surface and try to fix the opening or crack in the cable raceway in container six.

At 3:20 p.m. we surfaced, raised containers five and six and a party of specialists went on deck to investigate missile container six. Ten minutes later, the silhouettes of two Japanese trawlers appeared on the horizon on a course headed away from us and at 3:35 p.m. ESM reported a weak signal from a AN/APS-20 radar. I gave the command to make an emergency dive to avoid the aircraft. Captain Third Rank Tsimbalenko and Captain Second Rank Bayburin reported that the inspection was complete. Everything was whole with no defects, meaning that there was no visible cause of the leak. Thirty minutes later water again came through the drain valve in compartment seven. I decided to surface again in order to deal with the leak. Captain Second Rank Bayburin suggested wrapping the flange joint with bindings impregnated with epoxy. At 8:00 p.m. we surfaced and carried out his suggestions and *also transmitted a report to shore about the leak in missile container six. We received the following intelligence report:*

> "The strike carriers Coral Sea, Kitty Hawk *and*
> Constellation *are located 190 miles north of Da Nang.
> The strike carrier* Midway *is east of Saigon with for-
> ty-seven vessels in support. The carriers flew 369 sorties
> in a twenty-four hour period, 279 strike sorties. In the
> last twenty-four hours ships of the U.S. Seventh Fleet
> joined by bombers struck port structures with bombs
> and gunfire in Haiphong and Kam-Pha, the island of
> Kak-Ba, and the Do-Shon Peninsula. As a result of
> the bombardment in Kam-Pha, the Soviet merchant
> ship* G. Akopyan *was set on fire. The helicopter carrier*
> Okinawa *with an accompanying amphibious group is
> located 180 miles north of Da Nang."*

*On 12 May water again began to come out of the cable race-
way in container six through the drain valve in compartment seven.
Accordingly I made the decision to continue the patrol at depths no
greater than eighty meters.*[33]

*At 6:00 a.m. we passed abeam of Ulin-Do. At 12:00 a.m., I came
to periscope depth to determine our position. There were up to fifty
Japanese trawlers on a bearing of 120 to 250 degrees on the horizon at a range of seven miles. The Navigation Officer, Captain Third
Rank V.Voronin reported that the depth finder went out of service.*

---

[33] *This was a surprise to Captain Minton and showed how an assumption can lead to
a dangerous situation. Because there was no accurate method to determine the actual
keel depth of another submarine, he assumed that K 184 was usually operating at one
hundred meters. He then operated Guardfish at depths above and below that depth
to reduce the potential of collision. With the K 184 running at eighty meters we were
often at the same depth. Captain Minton said, "Sometimes it just pays to be lucky."*

The Navigator determined our position using the sun, Loran Alfa, and Loran Charlie.[34]

At 4:34 a.m., we got the depth finder working again and thankfully passed abeam of a bank with depths ranging from nine to thirty meters.

On board the *Guardfish*, my Executive Officer, Lieutenant Commander Larry Vogt, and I shared the command duty. I took the nights and he took the days. Without Larry, this trail would not have succeeded.

While on special operations, our practice was to shift night for day and use Greenwich time-zone (Zulu). That shift allowed most of our ship's noisy evolutions to be conducted when it was dark and when there was less Soviet naval activity. It also made it easier for us to keep our report logs in the required Greenwich time-zone rather than always converting time from the local time-zone. With the exception of the Officer of the Deck, the Assistant Officer of the Deck, and the plotting teams, the remainder of the crew was in four sections standing six hour watches.

One submarine is hard to trail, three or four is impossible. Therefore we focused our efforts on maintaining contact with the Echo II we had visually identified while hoping to remain undetected. Later I was to learn that the U.S. fixed underwater sonar array system called SOSUS, an acronym for Sound Surveillance System, had confirmed that four Soviet submarines deployed from the Sea of Japan.

When the Echo II we were trailing resumed its transit toward the Tsushima Straits I had two important decisions to make.

First decision: Did the deployment of three, possibly four, Soviet submarines meet the requirement for breaking radio silence? I later learned that four submarines had deployed from Vladivostok and one deployed from Petropavlovsk. This was one more Soviet submarine

---

[34] *By email Captain Minton asked about our celestial navigation capability at periscope depth. He told me that Guardfish did not have that capability. I replied, "We could fix our position by using an astronavigation periscope (called Lyre), which allowed us to measure the height of stars, sun, and moon. Position was then determined with the help of a star globe, tables, a micro-calculator, and a sea astronomical year-book."*

than estimated by U.S. Naval Intelligence. The number one priority of all submarine surveillance operations was to provide an early warning of a significant deployment of Soviet Naval vessels. This type of report, called a "critic" report, had never been sent before by any U.S. submarine on a Cold War patrol. Breaking radio silence was a hazardous practice for any submarine on a covert operation and something no submariner of that era wanted to do. The term 'the silent service' applied in more than one way.

The process by which we were required to communicate used a high frequency radio transmission. Although the transmission was compressed and encrypted, the very fact that we transmitted could be detected by the Soviet electronic intercept stations along their coast and identified as uniquely coming from a U.S. submarine. Therefore it was likely the Soviets would detect our transmission. Using intercepts from two or more stations they could plot where it had come from and possibly correlate it with the activity of their submarines. Submariners from their first days at submarine school are indoctrinated in the philosophy of stealth and silence. Now was the time for *Guardfish* to break that silence and notify her operational commander of the situation. We didn't want to do it, but that was a chance we had to take. Reporting the deployment of three, possibly four, Soviet submarines was clearly a requirement of my operations order. On the night of May 12, we came to periscope depth for five minutes and transmitted the "critic" message. Fortunately our transmission was not detected – at least we had no indication that the Echo II had been alerted to our presence.

Second decision: Should *Guardfish* abandon her surveillance mission in the Sea of Japan to continue the trail of the Soviet submarine as he left our assigned patrol area? The operations order was silent on this count, but it made sense to me that my administrative boss Commander Submarine Force U.S. Pacific Fleet (COMSUBPAC), and my operational boss Commander Seventh Fleet (COMSEVENTHFLT), (who was in charge of all U.S. naval forces in the Western Pacific including the naval forces operating off Vietnam) would want to know exactly where the Soviet submarines were going. I did not have the luxury of time to request and wait for permission so I invoked the submarine commanding officer's secret creed, "No guts, No hero ribbon." We were on our way hoping that we were going to be given permission!

THE TECHNIQUES OF TRAILING

Trailing in real life was not like the actions depicted in Tom Clancy's movie *The Hunt for Red October*. It is an extremely difficult task requiring the full attention of the Officer of the Deck, sonar operators, and the tracking team. Too close and you could be detected, too far away and contact could be lost.

In the first day or so of the trail there was a certain amount of concern over the proximity of the other three of four Soviet submarines. It seemed reasonable to me that they would operate independently as we would. Because of mutual interference concerns, the normal submarine practice would be to separate submarines in transit by a significant distance to allow them to transit safely. But there was also a possibility lurking in the back of my mind that they might work more like a World War II wolf pack with one submarine leaping ahead of the others and then lie in wait while checking for a U.S. submarine in trail as they passed. Such tactics would put me in a very difficult position, maintaining contact on one submarine while possibly overtaking another. This didn't turn out to be the case and my concern was unfounded, but it certainly gave me pause when we first started the trail heading south.

Trailing was an exciting experience. We were involved in something that we had practiced before deployment in a simulator for very short-term time frames, two to three hours. It was fortunate my fire control tracking team and I attended this training because we had learned and practiced a new technique called geographic plotting. Geographic plotting supplemented the older strip plotting technique which had been used for many years, as far back as World War II. Typically, active tracking only lasted at the most an hour. Now we were faced with trailing the Echo II for days and possibly weeks on end. Out of necessity, we shifted from a short duration fire control tracking team to one we developed on the fly, that could go twenty-four hours a day seven days a week. This was a big change in the way we operated.

We modified all of our ship routines based on the Echo II's behavior. Sanitary tanks were blown at shallow depths when contact was sufficiently strong to allow us to change from the deeper tracking depths of 245 or 409 feet. Flooding of the negative tank for trim purposes was also restricted to shallow depths in order to reduce the noise associated with that evolution. Because of the noise and excessive time required at shallow depths, the operation of the trash disposal unit (TDU) was suspended. All garbage was frozen (literally!) and all trash was compacted and stored in the number one auxiliary tank. At the time of our deployment submarines of our class did not have trash compactors. But before deploying from Pearl Harbor I had the Supply Officer buy a commercial trash compactor from Sears. It proved invaluable. After six months of extremely heavy use and many repairs by our ship's auxiliary men, including replacing the plastic internal pipes with stainless steel pipes, the compactor was really trashed. When we returned to Pearl Harbor I suggested that the Supply Officer return the compactor to Sears and ask for a new one. This was one of the only times I had an officer under my command refuse my orders. I even tried to convince him that he could explain the exceptional use the machine had endured and that I would be willing to sign a letter endorsing the compactors performance. No dice. So the compactor went off to be compacted itself in the shore dump.

Many of the crew members were reassigned to support the tracking party. New tracking team members were trained including members of the special surveillance group embarked for our planned operation in the Sea of Japan. This group was often referred to as "Spooks" because they would report aboard a submarine just before an operation and would leave as soon as the submarine returned to port leaving little or no trace of their presence. These electronics surveillance technicians and linguists needed an antenna above water to work their magic but because we were seldom at periscope depth during the trail there was little for them to do. The Spooks volunteered to assist where they could and became valuable assets to the tracking team.

The first few days of the trail we were playing a lot of catch-up. We had to learn how to best deal with the Echo II's maneuvers and how to best to use the people we had available. There were a lot of difficult hours put in while we were learning the tricks of trail. As the trail continued we got better at maintaining contact and the men who did the geographic plot became extremely proficient. In fact two of them got so good that they ultimately received medals for their contribution to the trail. These young men were Auxiliary Man of the Watch (Machinist Mate Second Class Thomas E. Cosgrove and Machinist Mate Second Class Thomas R. Lindberg) and would normally have not been assigned to the plotting team. But they were available and were intelligent and soon mastered the necessary plotting techniques. They became so proficient that I referred to the two of them as Aux of the Plot instead of Auxiliary Man of the Watch. They were truly amazing. Each Officer of the Deck (Chief Warrant Officer Frederick R. Heckel, Lieutenant Edward D. Bartell, and Lieutenant Richard C. Woodward) became exceptionally proficient in maneuvering *Guardfish* to maintain contact and provide the bearing rates necessary to calculate the Echo II's range. Junior Officers of the Deck Lieutenant (junior grade) Harold A. Williams, Lieutenant (junior grade) Lowell G. Lewis, and Lieutenant (junior grade) Michael Kovar were equally effective in supervising and training the plotting team.

For us to remain undetected, the Echo II's position, course, and speed had to be determined using passive sonar bearings. Passive ranging required *Guardfish* to frequently maneuver to generate a changing bearing to the contact. Because a trail like this is a twenty-four hour a day, seven days a week business, we had to establish additional tracking and plotting teams and arrange for their support. All activities on *Guardfish* were now focused on one priority, maintaining contact with the Echo II.

The tracking of a submarine is a full time task. There are many factors that affect how a trail is conducted – one of the most significant was the sonar conditions. By May 13, we were in an area of the

East China Sea transited by many merchant ships, all creating a tremendously high background noise level. In almost all of the Western Pacific the sonar conditions are also affected by a temperature layer typically located between one hundred twenty and one hundred forty feet. Submarines on opposite sides of the layer find it nearly impossible to maintain sonar contact. Thus, whenever we went to periscope depth to communicate or try to get a navigation fix we lost contact. We had to depend on the Echo II maintaining his course and speed and then trying to regain contact once we were both back on the same side of the layer. The same predicament applied when the Echo II went to periscope depth. Anytime we had to break contact was fraught with worry that the Echo II might do something unpredictable and we'd be unable to regain the trail.

When you watch some of the submarine movies like *The Hunt for Red October* they always seem to know what depth the other submarine is operating at. There was no system, automated or manual to truly determine the depth of the other submarine. The only time we were absolutely sure of the Echo II's depth was when he was at periscope depth and we actually saw him. Otherwise it was only a guess. There were times when we believed he was above the layer meaning that he was at least above one hundred forty feet and there were times when we believed he was below the layer. But we had no idea of his exact depth or if he was at a depth that would allow us to miss each other if we came too close. Although we tried to place ourselves at a depth where we least expected him to be operating, there was no assurance that we would not collide.

Submarines of that era had a sonar blind spot astern call the baffles. This blind spot is created by their hull masking sounds and interference caused by engineering machinery noises. The baffles are about 40 degrees wide, (20 degrees on either side of the stern). This area is larger on some submarine classes, smaller on others. Good submarine practice requires a submarine to turn periodically to allow their sonar to "see" into the baffle area and check for contacts astern. It is like looking into your rearview mirror.

Our priority was to maintain contact and to remain undetected by the Echo II. If we were detected it would jeopardize our mission and we might not be able to trail this submarine to its final destination. Loss of contact would deny our Operational Commander information needed to evaluate the threat this Soviet submarine posed to our forces off of the South Vietnamese coast. So we were very, very careful to prepare for each one of these baffle clearing maneuvers. U.S. submarine safety procedures required the trailing submarine to stay outside a minimum trailing range (MTR) calculated by using both the contact's and trailer's speeds. Because of the difficulty maintaining contact and the importance of this mission I elected to violate the MTR when necessary. As it turned out after a week in trail I received a message from COMSUBPAC granting me permission to do just that, trail inside the MTR if necessary. He must have been reading between the lines of my frequent Echo II position reports.

While trailing the Echo II, the MTR range was always posted in grease pencil on the front of the fire control panel. One day the officer in charge of the embarked special surveillance group while assisting the tracking team became concerned and drew me aside to point out that we were outside the MTR. Because we were so frequently inside that range he thought MTR meant the "maximum trailing range." We all got a good laugh at his expense.

In the *Hunt for Red October* they used the term "Crazy Ivan" for the Russian's baffle clearing maneuvers. I had never heard that term used in the Pacific, but we sure did gain plenty of experience (almost hourly) with the Echo II's turning to clear his baffles. Not counting major course changes, which were the equivalent to a baffle clearing maneuver, we experienced three hundred ten separate baffle clearing maneuvers during the trail. Sometimes it was a very passive turn of 90 degrees so that his sonar could listen for anything behind him and at other times he very aggressively turned 180 degrees and raced back at high speed along his previous track right at *Guardfish*. Doing this maneuver at high speeds was counterproductive because it limited their sonar's ability to hear and detect a trailer. I believed it was a sort of "devil may care" approach to baffle clearing and made me wonder if the object of this method was to find a trailer by Braille. I was extremely uneasy when this happened because we were, in fact, astern of them offset slightly on one side or the other. Since we were frequently within three thousand to four thousand yards our combined speeds during this maneuver had us initially closing at about eighteen knots with the potential for a collision in less than five minutes. Collision obviously would be the worst case scenario but there was also a decent chance they could detect our presence as the range closed.

I have to admit that some of the young sailors were pretty upset during baffle clearing maneuvers. When I looked around the control room sometimes I saw nothing but eyes as wide as saucers. The crew knew the situation was very serious and had a real element of danger. We had a couple of sailors and one officer who were unable to cope with trailing and could not do their jobs under these conditions. We reassigned them to other tasks to prevent them from freezing up or causing a problem during the trail. But by far the majority of the crew recognized that what we were doing was part of submarining.

During my command of *Guardfish*, in times of stress I borrowed a diversion from Red Auerbach, the famous Celtic's basketball coach. When Red Auerbach was sure that the game was won he would light up his victory cigar and settle back in his chair even if the game wasn't over. My crew recognized that when I lit that cigar I was confident the situation was under control and soon the tension in our control room would melt away. They had faith that I was going to keep them out of trouble. Their faith may have been misplaced because at times I had my fingers crossed. The fact we were able to stay as far as possible from the closing submarine and avoid detection and collision during each one of those really wild baffle clearing maneuvers was, at some level, down to just luck.

When the Echo II made a baffle clearing maneuver, *Guardfish* tried to anticipate which way he would turn so that we were slightly off of his track on the opposite side. Additionally, as soon as a maneuver was detected, *Guardfish* slowed immediately to be as silent as possible and to give us more time and distance for the Echo II to return to his previous course. Without the advantage of a quieter submarine and superior sonar we would not have been successful in this trail. Exciting? Yes. Scary? You bet!

Fortunately the Echo II helped us by frequently clearing baffles right on the hour and alternating the direction of their turn from left to right. We could then anticipate which way the Echo II was probably going to turn allowing us to position ourselves on his opposite quarter prior to the turn providing us with a little more space once he started the maneuver.

To keep track of the Echo II's course and speed throughout the trail we depended on the only piece of information readily available, bearing. To develop range we had to measure two different bearing rates. On each leg of this maneuver we would set a constant course and speed. Assuming that the contact maintained its course and speed we could then calculate a bearing rate for the contact. A second leg of bearing rate was required using another course. Knowing two bearing rates and our own position allowed us to determine the range between us and the Echo II by applying a mathematical process that was developed many years ago by a submariner named Joe Ekelund. This process is referred to as Ekelund ranging.[35]

The following sketch was drawn by Sonarman First Class Harold Wilson to recognize the tracking party's continuous use of the Ekelund ranging technique. This figure isn't the Lone Ranger. He is, of course, the Ekelund Ranger. The circular device on his hat band is a bearing rate calculator used in Ekelund ranging.

---

[35] Joe Ekelund, now a retired Rear Admiral, developed the mathematical solution to calculating a targets range in the 1950's. Ekelund ranging helped revolutionize modern undersea warfare and is now a household phrase in the submarine community. An established method still used by tacticians and in automated fire-control algorithms; it has long been part of the course of study in target motion analysis at the U.S. Naval Submarine School.

Developing bearing rate is not a simple process and is an important function of the plotting team. The team recorded sonar bearings every thirty seconds and plotted them on a time-bearing plot. This procedure enabled us to smooth out errors in sonar bearing and differences in sound propagation through the water which would affect the accuracy of the sonar bearing. The team corrected for these errors by taking a series of bearings over a period of time and smoothing the resulting to create a continuous bearing curve. The technical term for this in submarine tracking is 'fairing' the curve, where fair means to streamline. The slope of the time/bearing plot at a given time provided the targets bearing rate. Then with two legs of bearing rate, the range could be calculated. Every thirty seconds day and night during the whole trail members of the plotting team were reading a bearing and plotting it on a graph to determine the bearing rate and faired bearing. During a baffle clearing maneuver when we needed the information much more rapidly, bearings were taken every fifteen seconds. **Think about the intense effort that was required to focus on this process hour after hour, day after day, week after week.**

In fact, we ran into an unexpected problem. We didn't have enough plotting paper onboard. Early in the trail we realized at the present rate we were soon going to run out. To conserve plotting paper we used each sheet for multiple plots until it was too full to continue. Then it was taken down and a member of the off watch would sit and erase it. We used the plotting papers again and again until they were in such bad shape that they had to be discarded. The same thing was true of geographic plotting sheets. We were able to use them multiple times then turn the sheet over and use its back. Even then we nearly did not have enough paper to maintain the trail. In addition to the constant bearing rates, during some parts of the trail when water depth was less than two thousand five hundred fathoms and bottom contour was fairly smooth, sonar was able to measure the time difference between the Echo II's sound coming directly to us and his sound bouncing off of the bottom. Knowing the water depth we could calculate a fairly accurate range to the Echo II. This helped to confirm our calculated Ekelund bearing rate ranges.

Knowing the range and bearing was vital to handling baffle clearing maneuvers. As I have said the most used method was to immediately slow the submarine and maintain as narrow of an aspect toward him as possible in an effort to prevent him from picking up our engineering and propulsion noises. Ideally, we would be pointing our bow directly at the target to minimize the amount of sound that might reach him. Remember, however, that this is a three dimensional problem and we were largely unsure of where we stood in the third dimension. And once he started the turn you never knew how far he was going to turn. On *Guardfish* we rigged the ship for the quietest conditions possible, ultra-quiet, and manned the sound powered telephones in all spaces to alert the crew of the baffle clearing maneuver. Noise making activities such as maintenance, music being played, or almost any activities throughout the ship were stopped and collectively we all held our breathe during a baffle clearing maneuver. There were times when the Echo II came very close to us. Fortunately for us his sonar wasn't that good and his operators did not detect us.

The Echo II frequently cavitated. Cavitation is the rapid formation and collapse of bubbles caused by a submarine's propeller. If the submarine goes deeper or slows the possibility of cavitation is reduced. They did not always follow usual submarine practice allowing us to determine Echo II's speed by using his turns (revolutions/minute) to estimate his speed.

THE TRAIL CONTINUES

Now about eighteen hours into trailing the Echo II class in the East China Sea aboard the *Guardfish*, I had a new problem to address. During the initial time of this trail, *Guardfish* had been unable to receive all the messages sent to us on the submarine radio broadcast. In order to ensure that each submarine receives each assigned message, the messages are numbered and repeated hourly for eight hours. It was our responsibility to come to periscope depth to receive all message within that time frame. The Navigator and Communication Officers were upset that I had skipped the last available broadcast. My response was, "forget about that, and focus on the trail."

I understood their concern. We were blind and deaf. We still were unsure of our orders or whether we were alone in this trail. Were other U.S. submarines tracking those Soviet subs that also had left Vladivostok? Were they in fact enroute to Haiphong? Was there any intelligence as to their intentions? And was the Soviet Union still honoring its 'hands-off' policy as to the bombing of Vietnamese coastal waters? Without breaching radio silence, we had no way of knowing the situation in Vietnam and the South China Sea — a region engulfed in the fires of war.

No one had expected to be involved in an extended trail of a Soviet submarine. Maintaining contact with the Echo II greatly limited the time we could receive message traffic. Frequently when at periscope depth, *Guardfish* was separated from the Echo II by a thermal layer and unable to maintain any contact. Having received our 'critic' message, my boss, COMSUBPAC, anticipated my problem and assigned *Guardfish* to a special abbreviated broadcast carrying only messages screened for us and repeated for twenty-four hours. This broadcast change allowed *Guardfish* to come to periscope depth just once a day and was *our first and only acknowledgment* that leaving my assigned patrol area for the trail had been approved. What a relief.

Among the message we received was the word that during the last twenty-four hours, ships of the Seventh Fleet joined by bombers had struck port structures with bombs and gunfire in Haiphong, Kam-Pha, the Island of Kak-Ba, and the Do-Shon Peninsula, and had mined the harbors of Hanoi and Haiphong. As a result of this bombardment in Kam-Pha, the Soviet merchant ship *G. Akopyan* was set on fire. Such collateral damage was of serious concern to our mission and colored heavily the deployment of submarines from the Soviet base at Vladivostok.

———

Throughout all this, we still didn't know the Echo II's destination but we did have two valuable clues to determining his course at any given time. As *Guardfish* passed astern of the Echo II there were two distinct nulls in his radiated noise at 165 and 180 degrees from his bow. Sonar frequently could anticipate these nulls and provide the plotting team with a "Mark" when at the stern null. The bearing to the Echo II at that instant was set as the Echo II's course. Also the Echo II frequently set courses on cardinal headings (north, south, east, and west) further assisting our tracking team.

Though we did not know it, our actions were to continue for twenty-eight days, as the Echo II and *Guardfish* sailed on. It became clear, at this point, that the Russian commander had set his sights on the South China Sea.

═══

Late in the evening of May 12, the Echo II turned to the southeast on a base course of 125. This would take him south of Fukue Shima and into deeper water. I was grateful for his decision not to transit to the South China Sea via the Formosa Strait. The deep water of his course was well worth the longer transit.

In the morning of May 13, *Guardfish* came to periscope depth while the Echo II was also at a periscope depth and I sighted his periscope and communications masts, which was a relief. Once during previous special operation I had trailed all night what sonar thought was a Soviet diesel submarine either on the surface or submerged snorkeling. When the contact slowed and stopped I came to periscope depth. The contact then turned on his deck lights almost blinding me. It turned out we had been trailing a Japanese fishing boat. I wasn't going to make that mistake again and the sighting of the Echo II's masts confirmed that we still had our Echo II.

LOSS OF CONTACT

On the evening of May 13, the Echo II again came to periscope depth. At the time, I believed that the Echo II had remained at periscope depth for an extended period of time. However, after about fifty minutes, it became clear that we had lost contact. The Echo II had evidently gone deep and opened the range between us at nine knots while we thought he was still at periscope depth at five knots. This was the first big crisis of the trail. We could only guess his location based on his previous course. Any method of finding him would involve speeding up and sprinting after him, but unfortunately another characteristic of sonar is that as you increase your speed the range in which you can detect another contact is decreased radically by the interference of the noise of water flowing over the sonar dome.

In yet another fortuitous decision, prior to deploying from Pearl

Harbor we had filled in and fiberglassed over openings in the deck near the sonar dome on the bow above the surfaced water line. This unauthorized modification included covering the mounting hole for the jackstaff displayed by all U.S. Naval ships and submarines when in port. Our plan was to wing it and just not use the jackstaff, but after completing this fiberglass modification *Guardfish* was tied up adjacent to COMSUBPAC's headquarters in Pearl Harbor. This violation of procedure resulting in a rather nasty phone call to our Executive Officer to replace the jackstaff, immediately! We were forced to jury rig the jackstaff to the forward capstan. All the effort was worth it since our fiberglass modification reduced the flow noise level sufficiently to allow us to increase speed by almost two additional knots before we were noise limited. Thus we were able to successfully trail at higher speeds than before. Not all of our improvement projects worked out as well – at that same time my crew also covered the fairwater (sail) with fiberglass. But this project was a disaster and the fiberglass on the sail ripped off the first time we ran at full speed.

Another advantage we had was a cleaner hull and screw than most boats. The submarine base in Pearl Harbor had an air driven device which worked much like an underwater floor cleaner. But it seemed to always be either in use or broken so I had one purchased just for *Guardfish*. Almost every time we were in any port our divers used it to our advantage. There is nothing that divers want to do more than to get into the water. The cleaner the hull and screw, the less noise they generate as the boat transits underwater. As a result of our cleaning program, *Guardfish* was faster and quieter than her contemporaries. Prior to deployment we had also worked diligently correcting equipment noises and sound shorts. During the workup for the deployment to the Western Pacific we identified a significant sound tonal plaguing us while we were submerged and reducing our sonar effectiveness. We could tell that the sound was coming from outside of the hull and was caused by water flow over the hull. In port a sonarman and I rapped on various parts of the sail and superstructure with rubber mallets until we hit the snorkel exhaust diffuser plate on the after end of the sail and the sound it made was exactly the frequency we had been hearing on sonar. We then, again without authorization, cut about ten inches off both sides of the diffuser plate thus eliminating the flow vibration.

These efforts improved our sonar capability and played an important part in our successful trailing of the Echo II.

After losing contact with the Echo II our dilemma was how best to regain contact. If a contact has moved beyond your sonar detection range you might reasonably assume that he had continued down the track on his previous course. You can guess his speed, perhaps it was the speed that he had previously been using. The longer you wait and the slower you close his estimated position the further off those assumptions may be. It's important to close the contact as rapidly and safely as possible then slow and hopefully detect him. We used this "sprint and drift" tactic. We sprinted after him at twenty knots on a course just slightly to the west of his previous course. I did not want to overrun him at that speed and I had no idea what depth he was operating at and I wasn't really sure what bearing he was on. It was safer to not be right on his track if we caught up with him while at twenty knots. Flying blind after another submarine is not a very comforting practice.

CONTACT RECOVERED

The situation was tense. We needed some luck. After an hour and a half at twenty knots, I couldn't take the suspense any longer and I slowed *Guardfish* to six knots. Almost immediately we detected a very faint sonar contact on our port beam. We had almost run right past him! Sonar was able to identify by the sound characteristics that it was the Echo II. Within another half hour we closed into a comfortable trail position.

The following chartlet from *Guardfish's* patrol report shows the relative positions of the Echo II and *Guardfish* on May 13. The Echo II's track is the straight line and *Guardfish's* track is the squiggly line showing maneuvers required for Ekelund ranging. At 6:19 p.m. contact of the Echo II at periscope depth was lost and not regained until 10:00 p.m. The period using the "sprint and drift" tactic can easily be seen.

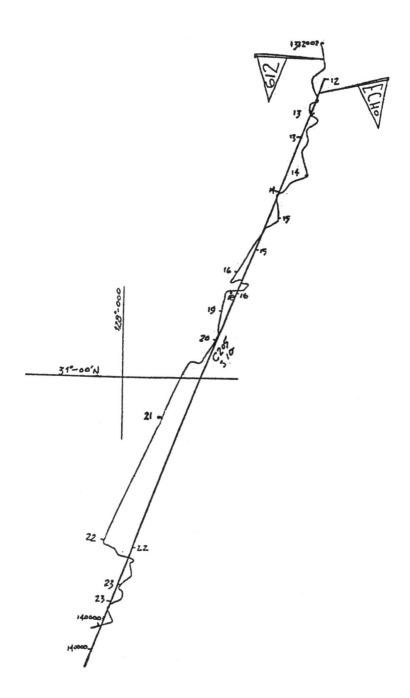

This was our first really critical trail error. Having lost him for three hours forty-one minutes, we were determined not to let that sort of thing happen again. Because of the sound conditions in that part of the ocean we were required to maintain a fairly tight trail — between three thousand and four thousand yards. Frequently during baffle clearing maneuvers we were well within three thousand yards.

The sonarman who reacquired the Echo II was *Guardfish's* best. All the sonar operators were good, but Sonarman First Class Harold K. Wilson had the best ears and played the sonar suite like a virtuoso. His performance as a sonar watch supervisor was outstanding. When I first watched the movie *The Hunt for Red October* and saw the Sonarman Second Class Ronald "Jonesy" Jones of the U.S. submarine *Dallas* depicted by actor Courtney B. Vance my first thought was "That's Wilson!"

"Willy" was our Jonesy. He was one of the first *Guardfish* crew members that I really got to know when I took command of the boat in Pascagoula, Mississippi. At the time, Wilson was dating and had fallen in love with a lovely Pascagoula girl, Ester, and they were planning their wedding. Wilson began the search for an apartment for them and was thwarted at every contact. He had a cultured British accent which he claimed came from living in Jamaica and many of his phone calls to landlords were positive. "Yes, Mr. Wilson we do have a nice apartment available." When they saw he was black they would not rent to him. Wilson went to my Executive Officer and explained his problem. The Executive Officer came to me to see what we could do. I called the President of the Pascagoula Shipyard and related to him Wilson's predicament. The Shipyard President asked that Wilson identify which two apartments he was most interested in and within the hour Wilson received calls from the two landlords saying, "I was mistaken, I do have an apartment for you." The shipyard was the only big business in the town and was all powerful. Soon afterward, Wilson and Ester were married in a little church in the black part of town accompanied by most of the *Guardfish* officers and crew in dress white uniforms. It caused quite a stir in the whole town especially those living in the community near the church. Many years later Wilson told me that some of the local men were upset that all those "white folk" were at their church, but when they saw that the officers were wearing dress swords they decided not to cause any trouble.

Regaining contact was so significant that I decided I needed to provide an immediate tangible reward to Wilson. What could I use? Then I remembered my wife had picked up a bag of colored smiley face pins for me before we left home port in Hawaii. I didn't know how Wilson or other members of the crew would react to this type of recognition. Was it too hokey? Was it something that they would think was childish or ridiculous? A submarine crew was made up of young men and their attitudes were those of young men. The average age of my crew was in the early twenties and many of them were much younger. To be recognized contributing to a major event was exciting and really motivating to them and the smiley buttons were what I had, so I took the chance. I called Wilson to the control room and with a few words on the ships announcing system (1MC) I pinned a smiley button on his chest. It turned out that Wilson and the whole crew loved it. The smiley pins became an important device for me. Over the next several weeks I recognized various accomplishments of "above and beyond the call of duty" for members of the crew, including two auxiliary men (Machinist Mate Second Class Thomas E. Cosgrove and Machinist Mate Second Class Thomas R. Limberg) who became the most proficient trail plotters that the Navy ever had, a radioman (Chief Radioman Arthur O'Meally) for his expertise in handling the critical communications and setting up the slot buoys, a cook (Commissaryman Second Class Robert Hicks) for the best damn sticky buns this skipper had ever eaten, and to many more members of my crew, officer and enlisted, whose dedication and expertise made this trail possible. They all wore their pins proudly for the remainder of the cruise. So many sonar men were recognized that I finally awarded a large four inch diameter smiley pin to the sonar room. The sonarmen mounted it on the sonar room door.

About this time we received a message from COMSEVENTHFLT directing us to an appendix of the Seventh Fleet Operations Order for our Rules of Engagement. We did not have, nor were we required to have, that appendix on board. This was a small inconvenience and I just focused on maintaining the trail. Several days later the

COMSUBFLOT SEVEN intelligence staff in Yokosuka, Japan, realized that our classified publications load list did not include the referenced appendix and they sent us the applicable parts of the Rules of Engagement by message. Basically the rules said if the Echo II launches his missiles *Guardfish* was to send a message. This was not much help to me because if the Echo II closed our fleet to within his missile range and launched he was committing an act of war and I did not need any more direction to do my duty. Someone back at Seventh Fleet headquarters was just covering his ass.

LIMITED NAVIGATIONAL CAPABILITY WHILE TRAILING

Navigation in those days was much more difficult than it is now. To navigate we needed to go to periscope depth. Unfortunately, when we went to periscope depth we would lose contact with the Echo II if he was below the thermal layer. Therefore we tried to limit the time we were at periscope depth to just those periods necessary to copy our broadcast. We were required to copy our radio broadcast at least once every twenty-four hours. If the timing worked out we might be able to get a navigational fix from LORAN-A, a land based system, or NAVSAT, the only navigation satellite system that existed at that time. NAVSAT required you to be at periscope depth exactly when the satellite was passing over. Broadcast and satellite pass times frequently didn't match at all. Because the reception of LORAN-A signals in the Western Pacific was extremely poor they provided us with some input but not of sufficient quality for us to upgrade our inertial navigation system. Unfortunately, the Submarine Inertial Navigation System (SINS) was of absolutely no use unless it was provided with frequent updates. It has been said that "SINS is only good enough to tell you where you are after you've told it where it was." Not much help when navigational input was very infrequent. The Worldwide Global Positioning System (GPS) coverage was not established until many years later. Therefore we basically depended upon the Echo II for navigation — relying on the fact that if we were close enough to them, their navigation would keep us away from underwater obstructions.

Chartlet of the trail in the East China Sea

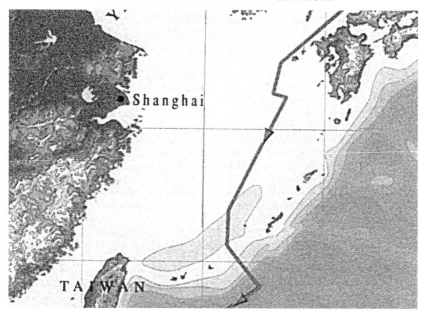

TRANSITING FROM THE EAST CHINA SEA TO THE PHILIPPINE SEA

On 15 May we entered the Philippines Sea. We received a message giving us a patrol area in the South China Sea designated number one. The area was similar in shape to a coffin lid. K 45 was given area two, an area with a lot of bars and banks. We were ordered to be prepared to use conventional weapons on command and in self-defense. That night I received information from Political Officer Kuz'min who said that he condemns the aggression by the United States in Vietnam. This was "very important" information for the boat.

On the morning of May 15, the seriousness of our dependence on the Echo II's navigation was underscored as we proceeded south into the East China Sea. The Echo II turned southeast just south of Okinawa to transit into the Philippine Sea. I believed that he had turned too soon and might not clear one of the small islands south of Okinawa. In fact I was so sure that the Echo II had cut the corner dangerously close I positioned *Guardfish* on his starboard quarter further to the south and in deeper water. I alerted sonar to the possibility that we might actually hear the Echo II run aground as he passed Kume Shima Island. It didn't turn out that way. He obviously had a more accurate position than we did and it pointed out how dependent we were on his navigation.

I understood that frequent updates of position, course, and speed were needed ashore to assess the threat and intent of the Soviet forces. I didn't know at the time but I suspected that our reports were being sent to the highest level of government. I was later told that President Nixon and his National Security Advisor, Henry Kissinger, were briefed by an old friend and shipmate Captain George Vahsen. George told me later that he went to the White House daily with the latest information from *Guardfish* in a locked briefcase.

16 May. We continued to travel to the designated area after passing Okinawa and we only came to periscope depth twice to get the broadcast. I called the missile officer, Captain Third Rank Tsimbalenko, to the control room. Out of all the watch officers Tsimbalenko was the most prepared, the best educated, and he knew the missile systems like no one's business. He reported that everything was normal in container six and the water flow from the cable raceway wasn't increasing.

17 May. Sea state was three with swells, fog, and tropical rain. We fixed our position using Loran Alpha and Charlie, and also got a radar fix. From the intelligence summary:

> *"A cruiser and destroyer left the Tonkin Gulf in the direction of Saigon. Nixon plans to be in Moscow for talks on the 25 May. The intensity of military activity in Vietnam has significantly decreased."*

18 May. Today the Electronics Material Officer, Captain Third Rank V.F. Tereshchenko, outlined his plan to search for enemy surface ships and submarines in area number one as well reporting on the bathythermograph (BT) data [36] *and possible measures that could be used to mask our boat from enemy ASW forces.*

19 May. Today we conducted a check of all the emergency escape gear on the boat. A couple of discrepancies were discovered, but they were quickly rectified.

TECHNIQUES USED TO REPORT THE ECHO II'S MOVEMENTS

There are several methods by which a submarine can communicate. Earlier I mentioned the high frequency (HF) short duration transmission that we used to report our initial detection of the Soviet deployment. There are other HF radio transmission types that provide us with a more conventional means to communicate, much like those used by most U.S. naval surface ships of that era. This method is a step–up from hand keying Morse code in that it basically sent an encrypted message on teletype through an HF transmitter. This method was called ORESTES, the code word for the encryption device. ORESTES's drawbacks were that it was both detectable and time consuming; the advantage was that the transmissions were not uniquely identifiable as coming from a submarine. However, because of the high volume of radio traffic from the war zone it took a long time to transmit any message and frequently it was very difficult to even contact the U.S. Naval Communication Station in the Philippines in order to transmit our messages. Even when we used Flash priority, the highest priority available in the U.S. communication system, we were frequently not able to get on the message queue. The most reliable and preferred method for us to communicate was ultrahigh frequency (UHF), which is a line of sight transmission and only detectable at a very close range. My Submarine Force Commander, having recognized our communication difficulty, provided us with a P-3 anti-submarine patrol aircraft flying secret

---

[36] *A bathythermograph is an instrument that records water temperature in relation to ocean depth. It is frequently used by submarines to determine the layer depth and identify the best operating depth to remain undetected.*

missions in the general vicinity of our position which permitted us the option of two UHF communication techniques. The first method was for *Guardfish* to come to periscope depth and actually transmit a UHF message directly to the aircraft using NESTOR, a code word for a device which encrypted voice transmission. The other method was to eject a slot-buoy while fully submerged. A slot buoy is a small radio transmitter that can be launched out of the submarine's signal ejector with a prerecorded message. It floats to the surface, transmits the message multiple times, and ultimately sinks. In both methods, after receiving the message, the P-3 aircraft would fly back to their base in the Philippines and covertly forward the message through the naval communications system back to Washington, D.C. Returning to the base ensured that their retransmission of our message could not be correlated to *Guardfish's* or the Echo II's position. This practice worked well and the Soviets were never alerted by our electronic emissions.

While we were sending messages we were also receiving messages of encouragement. My practice was to pass along this praise to the crew by reading these messages over the ships announcing system (1MC) when conditions permitted. I would generally start by saying "We have received another Atta-boy" followed by the relevant parts of the message. The crew responded well to this unsolicited praise. They were proud of what they were doing. The following are unclassified portions of two messages received during the trail:

> "In the face of poor sonar conditions and under the stress of knowing that your actions played a significant role in the evaluation of the Soviet response to the decision to mine North Vietnam ports, you have demonstrated magnificent performance. Although the extent of your personal contribution during this tense period may never be public, the performance of the team in *Guardfish* under protracted and difficult conditions has been acknowledged and appreciated at all levels of our government. Your professionalism and persistence under trying conditions have been in

the highest traditions of the naval service. I am proud of your signal accomplishments and congratulate you and everyone in *Guardfish* on a job well done."

Rear Admiral P. L. Lacy Jr., COMSUBPAC

"Your complete understanding of your mission, national priorities, and knowledge of the overall political situation demonstrates an awareness and professionalism which is heart-warming. The demonstrated competence of you and your crew is in the highest standards of the naval service and speaks well of the readiness of the submarine service. Well Done."

Admiral B. A. Clarey, CINPACFLT

During the trail, I had a chair placed in the control room between our two periscopes. It could easily be removed when we were coming to periscope depth so as not to interfere with the operation of the periscopes. This gave the Executive Officer and me a place to sit while we monitored the maneuvering of the submarine and the performance of the plotting team. One day when I went to the control room I found a dymo-tape label placed on the chair's back reading "AT'TA BOY CAPT'N." I still have the tape and treasure it.

In addition to the chair, I had an open microphone and receiver installed connecting the control room directly to the sonar room. This allowed me and members of the watch team to talk to the sonar supervisor without using a telephone handset. This arrangement was extremely helpful when the Echo II cleared baffles. Sonar was the first to detect any of the Echo II's maneuvers and could frequently measure his direction and speed change by doppler shift. The sonar supervisor was able to talk directly to the Officer of the Deck and the plotting team describing what he was hearing and seeing on his many displays.

U.S. Pacific Submarine Force Response to the Soviet Submarine Deployment

During this period of the trail all hell was breaking loose in Pearl Harbor. In response to the Soviet submarine deployment that we had reported, the Commander in Chief of the U.S. Pacific Fleet directed Commander Submarine Force U.S. Pacific Fleet to scramble (immediately deploy) every available nuclear attack submarine in the Pacific. They were all sent to the Western Pacific, specifically to the South China Sea to provide protection for our surface forces and to try to locate the other Soviet submarines. The increase in submarine traffic created a tremendous problem for our type commander's submarine staff. Because it was difficult for U.S. submarines to detect each other, the staff had to position our submarines so that they would not interfere with each other and to prevent the possibility of collision between two ships of our own Navy. To get them to the South China Sea they all had to transit the Bashi Channel located north of Luzon between Luzon and Taiwan, an enormous traffic management challenge.

Five Soviet submarines and a dozen or more U.S. submarines created a real problem for me. I had to stay with the Echo II Soviet submarine and I was restricted in my ability to communicate while maintaining the trail. When we updated the Echo II's position, course, and speed the submarine type commander's staff had to relocate the other U.S. submarines to get them out of our path. This was made more difficult because of the time delay of getting a message to our submarines when they were not at periscope depth.

Guardfish was committed to going wherever the Echo II went and the staff had to relocate the deploying submarines frequently as position updates were received to ensure that the much quieter U.S. submarines would not endanger each other or *Guardfish.*

Once in the Philippine Sea, the Echo II turned southwest heading in the general direction of the Bashi Channel. This channel is the usual northern entrance to the South China Sea. I was sure that this was his objective, but as we approached the channel the Echo II's track continued to the south of the normal entrance. The Echo II's course indicated he might intend to pass into the South China Sea just north of Batan Island. There are several other smaller channels between small islands north of Luzon. All of these channels were much narrower and much shallower than the Bashi Channel. It was possible that the Soviets had chosen this unlikely path if they suspected a U.S. anti-submarine barrier patrol in the vicinity of the Bashi Channel. I was concerned that a submerged trail of the Echo II through one of these smaller channels might be too hazardous to attempt.

Luckily I didn't have to make that decision. Early on the morning of May 17 the Echo II slowed, came to periscope depth and then, for the first time during the trail, went active on his fathometer, first on a short scale which was not suitable for the depth of water, and then on a longer scale which could get a return from the bottom. I concluded that he was lost! And we had been depending on his navigational ability!

While at periscope depth he must have gotten a good fix because the Echo II soon went deep, turned on a course to the Bashi Channel, and increased speed to sixteen knots. Having reported this rapid course and speed correction by slot buoy, I rushed after him knowing that repositioning of our submarines out of my way would be nearly impossible on this short notice. Additionally the upper signal ejector door did not close on the first try meaning there was a good chance that the slot buoy I used had been damaged and my message might not be received.

What could I do to protect *Guardfish* from a possible collision with a U.S. submarine and continue to maintain the trail? As an extra precaution against collision, I changed my depth to one hundred meters, a depth that I knew U.S. submarines would avoid. Our submarine force believed that the Soviets commonly operated at even metric depths, assuming such depths as one hundred meters and one hundred fifty meters would be popular. In World War II our submarines frequently operated fifty feet or one hundred feet, nice easy round numbers. I was sure our submarines would avoid operating at one hundred meters. So I ran at one hundred meters. Although I thought the Echo II was probably also operating at that depth I knew where he was and could try to maintain a safe distance. Because I did not know if any of our submarines were close to the Bashi Channel, this seemed like a prudent course of action. My apprehension was justified when we detected a U.S.

submarine clearing our track to the north at high speed. Incidentally, we later determined that this U.S. submarine detected neither of us as we passed close to the south and appeared to be undetected by the Echo II.

THE ECHO II ENTERED THE SOUTH CHINA SEA

On May 18, the Echo II entered the South China Sea, turned south, and commenced a transit to a point approximately three hundred miles off the coast of Luzon, between Luzon and the Paracel Islands.

Chartlet of the Trail from Philippines Sea to the South China Sea

For the next eight days he established a slow moving grid track which covered a rectangular holding area.

The following charlet from my patrol report shows one day of the typical maneuvering conducted by the Echo II in the South China Sea holding area. The squiggly line reflects *Guardfish's* maneuvers to generate bearing rates for Ekelund ranging.

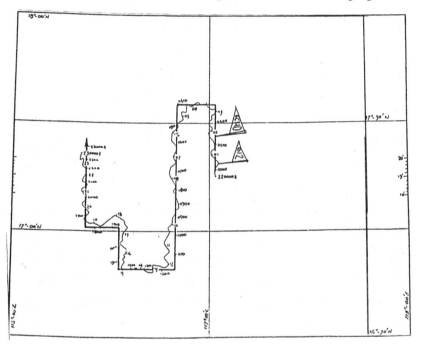

FROM OPPOSITE SIDES OF THE PERISCOPE

This charlet shows the composite of all the maneuvers
conducted by the Echo II in the South China Sea
holding area from May 18 through May 26.

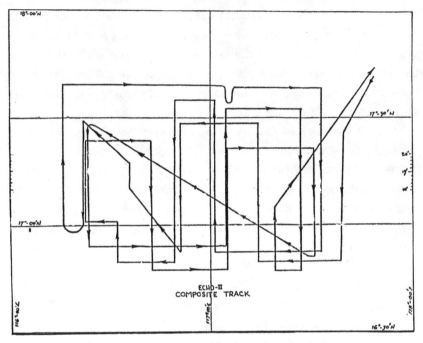

ECHO-II
COMPOSITE TRACK

This area was approximately seven hundred miles from Yankee
Station, the U.S. naval war zone, used by our carriers and other surface forces along the Vietnamese coast and was well beyond the two
hundred mile range of his Shaddock missiles. It was apparent that he
was placed there in a safe holding area to immediately respond if the
U.S. – USSR situation was to seriously escalate.

We were able to communicate the boundaries of his holding area,
his location, and his behavior to the chain of command. For example
on May 20 our sonar detected a U.S. destroyer's active sonar echo
ranging. The destroyer was heading east through the Echo II's holding
area probably enroute to Subic Bay, Philippines. After about two hours
the Echo II evidently heard the destroyer's echo ranging, increased
speed to sixteen knots, and opened thirty miles to the north. While in

the South China Sea he continued to display a passive posture avoiding any possible contact.

During this period for the first time since the beginning of the trail I was finally able to walk around the submarine and assess how the crew was doing. I was really impressed with what I saw. Every effort was taken to keep noise down. For example, in the crew's head, I found that each of the stall's stainless steel doors had sponges taped over the door jam, preventing the metal doors from slamming. I realized that this trail was truly a team effort.

On 20 May we took station in area number one. We came to periscope depth at 8:30 a.m. to catch the broadcast and fix our position. Immediately, dead ahead at a range of ten cables,[37] I saw an American auxiliary ship heading directly at us. We filled the emergency dive tank and dove to a safe depth. Sonar didn't hear the ship. The bathymetry was bad. Generally we didn't hear anything. Therefore every surfacing or trip to periscope depth was potentially dangerous due to the possibility of collision with a surface vessel.

On 22 May we detected an ASW P-3 Orion's AN/APS-80 radar, weak signal strength. We diverted course away from the aircraft.

On 23 May we came to periscope depth at 8:30 a.m. to catch the broadcast and a position fix. Political information was received, "Fleet Komsomol activities were held."[38] Not one word more was sent. Of course, it was "very important" information for a submarine in the South China Sea. We detected an ASW P-3 Orion's AN/APS-80 radar, weak signal strength. We diverted course away from the aircraft.

President Nixon Goes to Moscow

On 24 May we received instructions along with K 45 and K 7 to report our positions. We sent our latitude/longitude at 12:00 a.m. We had to

---

[37] Soviet Navy frequently uses cables to measure short distances. One cable is seven hundred twenty feet or two hundred nineteen yards.

[38] *Fleet Komsomol activities are performed by the Young Communist League. All Soviet submarines sailors and young officers were members of this organization. Other (more senior) officers were members of the Communist Party.*

send the message three times because atmospheric conditions in the area were bad. From the intelligence summary:

"Nixon is holding talks in Moscow."

We detected a weak signal from a AN/APS-20 radar carried on a P-2 Neptune ASW aircraft and diverted course away from the aircraft. The last two AN/APS-20 radar intercepts were analyzed and we came to the conclusion that the aircraft was conducting an ASW search.

On May 24, while the Echo II's track was close to the northern boundary of his holding area, sonar reported a possible second Soviet submarine operating to the north. I believe that one of the other Soviet submarines which we had detected leaving the Sea of Japan was patrolling just to the north. It was possible that their submarine holding areas were lined up north along the western coast of Luzon.

On 25 May sometime after lunch, the Engineer Officer, Captain Second Rank M.S. Bayburin, reported that there was a leak of refrigerant from the circulation pump of the first circuit of the port side reactor and I made the decision to turn it off since a buildup of the levels of radioactive gases and aerosols had begun in compartment six.

While we were struggling hour by hour to maintain contact with the Echo II, world events were moving in a more peaceful direction. After long negotiations, President Nixon was able to travel to Moscow for a historic summit meeting with Soviet General Secretary Brezhnev. I was later told that on May 24, during that summit meeting, National Security Advisor Kissinger met privately with Brezhnev and informed Brezhnev that our Naval Forces knew that the Soviets had deployed submarines to the South China Sea and that the U.S. thought their presence so close to the Vietnamese War Zone was provocative and extremely dangerous. Although on *Guardfish* we were not aware of this conversation, within two days of this confrontation, on May 26, the Soviets blinked. The Echo II submarine left his patrol area and started to transit north toward the Bashi Channel.

The Echo II Departs the South China Sea

During the first day on the trail north sonar gained contact on another submerged submarine, bearing 089 degrees at a range of eight-thousand-two-hundred yards. The contact was also classified as a Soviet HEN class. Twelve minutes later we lost contact bearing 124 degrees, on course 180, speed nine knots. It surprised me later when I learned that no other of the U.S. attack submarine sent to the South China Sea detected any of the Soviet submarines deployed during this critical period. We seemed to attract them.

The trail north with the Echo II was a relief to me and the crew of *Guardfish*. We had been under extreme pressure and the idea that he might be heading back to Vladivostok to conclude his patrol was appealing. We were tired! The constant pressure of the trail was taking its toll on the ship in multiple ways. For instance, we were running low on oxygen candles, the device used on *Guardfish* to replenish oxygen for our atmosphere. From the very beginning of the trail I could predict the exact date we would have to break trail by the number of oxygen candles we had on board and the amount of oxygen we had in our emergency oxygen banks.

During the trail we also had to deal with several mechanical failures. One failure was to the hydraulic seal for the rudder ram. The rudder ram hydraulically positioned the rudder and we were unable to stop and replace the seal. The Engineer Officer, Lieutenant Commander William B. Byers, came up with a unique and practical solution. The hydraulic oil leaking from the seal was collected in a large drip pan and routed through a temporary pipe to an oil purifier and then to a hydraulic storage tank. Replacement oil for the hydraulic system was then pumped back to the system as needed. As long as the seal leak didn't get much worse we could continue the trail. Watchstanders were assigned to monitor this Rube-Goldberg fix.

On 26 May at 2:00 a.m., when we came to periscope depth, I immediately saw a 10,000 ton displacement ship dead ahead, range ten cables. Sonar didn't hear anything. We made an emergency dive to a

safe depth. In the next broadcast we got a message from shore ordering
us to return to base.

On May 26 while at periscope depth, I sighted and photographed
the Echo II's masts.

**This photograph was taken through our periscope showing
the Echo II's masts (Periscope with fairing, STOPLIGHT ESM
mast, and a HF antenna). The view is of a 169 degree starboard
angle on the bow, range three-thousand-six-hundred yards.**

We still appeared to be heading back toward Vladivostok, a relief
to the whole crew. Unfortunately the Echo II had other orders.

*At night on 27 May we received a message canceling the order to
return to base. Instead they gave us an order to take up a new position
in the Philippines Sea which was in the shape of a circle with a radius
of thirty miles. They didn't say what we were to do in that circle. K 57
and K 189 also received water space in the Philippines Sea. We passed
through the Bashi Strait and fixed our position visually using an island.
During the broadcast, we detected a radar operating in single sweep*

mode, bearing 172 degree relative. In the periscope, the horizon was clear. We couldn't determine the parameters of the radar. I started the tracking board with the goal of identifying our pursuer during every periscope depth excursion. On it I noted the incoming messages, the weather, visual observations, and our maneuvering. It was possible that the radar was a BPS-9 belonging to a U.S. Permit class nuclear attack boat.

ECHO II's NEW PATROL AREA IN THE PHILIPPINE SEA

After transiting the Bashi Channel and sailing north, the Echo II established another patrol area in the Philippine Sea south of Okinawa. This particular piece of ocean had some of the worst possible acoustical properties. It was often crossed by merchant traffic and at night the ocean's biological noise and frequent rain showers were sometimes blinding to sonar. Maintaining contact became even harder than before, making it necessary for us to trail at closer and closer ranges.

LOST AND REGAINED CONTACT AGAIN

Early on May 27 the Echo II went to periscope depth and we lost contact with him for about one hour and twenty minutes. Soon he went to periscope depth again and we were having a very difficult time tracking him. Only a single tonal was available and contact was very tenuous. I decided to come up to periscope depth to improve the sonar conditions. That did not work out. It became apparent while we were at periscope depth that the Echo II had opened the range between us at twelve to fourteen knots on course 065. The tonal we thought we were tracking was coming from our own ship. I decided to sprint ahead for an hour at twenty-two knots to catch up to his dead reckoning position in hopes of regaining contact. One hour later I slowed to ten knots and regained contact on the Echo II, bearing 074, making three-hundred-sixty RPM on both screws. The contact was still very difficult to maintain. His range was about twenty-six- thousand yards and he was averaging fourteen knots.

Again I sprinted ahead to close the range. Just after sunset we had closed the Echo II and were trailing him at a comfortable range of four-thousand-seven-hundred yards. We had completely lost contact for two hours and forty-eight minutes. Much like our first experience of lost contact on May 13, this was a hair raising and stressful day!

The following chartlet is a composite of the Echo II's holding area in the Philippine Sea from 28 May to 6 June 1972. Note the track on May 28 begins to look like a holding area, but then the Echo II moved off to the east and after some more zigzagging establishes a circular holding area of about a fifty mile radius.

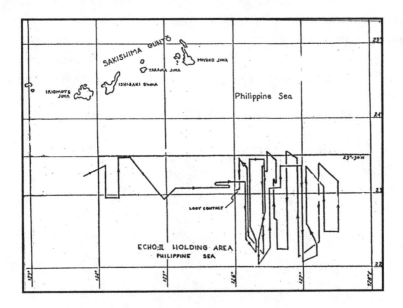

28 May. We took station in the Philippines Sea. Two messages were received in which there was an order to take another new area in the form of a circle with a radius of fifty miles. Also it was reported that it had been leaked to the American press that Soviet submarines were discovered in the South China Sea. Admiral N.I. Smirnov, the Commander of the Soviet Pacific Ocean Fleet, calls upon us to maintain our covert posture and curses K 57 for reporting the fact that he took station. Covertness was lost by Headquarters during our workups for deployment. The transit route was available to anyone who wasn't lazy, all the boats set out on the same route.

They ordered us to report our position by radio and there wasn't any sort of cover story created to cover the departure from our base. While at periscope depth to receive the broadcast we detected a radar operating in single sweep mode, bearing 170 degree relative. The horizon was clear. We weren't able to determine the pulse repetition frequency (PRF) or the pulse duration since the radar operated only three seconds. Again it is possible that it was a BPS-9 radar carried by a Permit class SSN.[39]

29 May. We took a position in the new area speed six knots, with no explicit mission. I made the decision to begin a search for American and Japanese surface ships. During the broadcast, we detected a radar operating in single sweep mode, bearing 175 degrees relative. The horizon was clear. We weren't able to determine the pulse repetition frequency (PRF) or the pulse duration since the radar operated only five seconds.

Chartlet of Trail from the South China Sea to the Philippine Sea

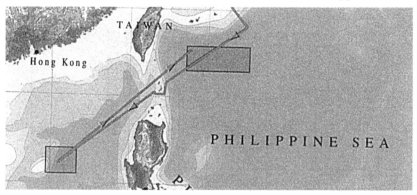

On 30 May, during the broadcast, we detected a radar operating in single sweep mode, bearing 175 degrees relative. The horizon was clear. I heard out a suggestion from the Executive Officer and Combat Systems Officer on how to flush out the foreign submarine and break off contact.

On May 30, we had another challenging casualty. The Mark 130

---

[39] Admiral Berzin mentions several times detecting a radar signal that he suspects is coming from a Permit class submarine like *Guardfish*. The signal was definitely not coming from *Guardfish* because the radar was de-energized throughout the patrol.

Computer failed — part of our fire control system, it could calculate automatic target motion analysis and rough instantaneous bearing rate. Despite our best efforts we were unable to fix this computer. Although automatic target motion analysis was more rapid than the methods used by the plotting team it was never as accurate. The Echo II's maneuvers continued to be analyzed by the plotting team using the slower manual techniques of the geographic plot and the time bearing plot. But this failure made early detection of speed changes difficult when the Echo II was not cavitating.

Sonarman First Class Harold K. Wilson (our Jonsey) drew this cartoon to depict the horrible sonar conditions in the Philippine Sea.

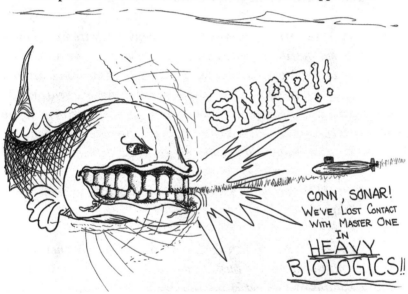

On 31 May, we got a message on the broadcast ordering us to yet another area and also received word that supposedly the U.S. found out about the locations of all of our boats in the South China Sea. Other areas were assigned to K 7, K 45 and K 57. The transit lane to these areas border some reefs and bars. The Soviet Pacific Fleet Command reminded us about navigational safety. We received an intelligence summary:

> *"The ASW carrier* Ticonderoga *was approaching the Philippines Sea. President Nixon flew to Iran and his Secretary of Defense had given the order to shut down the Safeguard Anti-Ballistic Missile Systems."*

On 1 June, during the broadcast, we detected a radar operating in single sweep mode, bearing 175 degrees relative. The horizon was clear. We received an intelligence summary:

> *"The ASW carrier* Ticonderoga *arrived in Guam for refueling. There are three CVAs in the Gulf of Tonkin and one CVA to the east of Saigon."*

On 2 June we carried out a special maneuver to attempt to flush out the U.S. submarine that was possibly following us. We didn't find anything. That day we came to periscope depth for the broadcast and we observed a ten thousand ton displacement transport bearing 280 degrees true, range forty cables. Sonar didn't detect anything before coming to periscope depth because of the bad acoustics conditions.

On 3 June we read in the intelligence summary:

> *"The ASW carrier* Ticonderoga *is transiting to the Philippines."*

K 45 was ordered to transit the Bashi Straits to occupy new water, once again past the bars and reefs. And again we received the warnings about navigation from Fleet Headquarters. Soon we will have spent a whole month at sea, splitting atoms for no apparent reason, although they could have given us the task of searching for and following a carrier. For a month we had cruised at six knots hearing and seeing nothing.

On 4 June, Intelligence summary:

> *"The ASW carrier* Ticonderoga *is entering the Luzon Strait."*

On 5 Jun, Intelligence summary:

"The ASW carrier Ticonderoga *has arrived in port, Subic Bay."*

I called the department heads together to discuss the patrol report. I warned them that I didn't want any whitewashing and to write what actually happened.

GUARDFISH'S PERISCOPE IS SIGHTED

On 6 June my administrative boss, COMSUBPAC, having recognized our oxygen limitation planned to have us pass our Soviet contact to another U.S. submarine. This maneuver had never been done before, even in controlled practice with submarines of our own force. A lengthy and dangerous procedure had been drafted by the staff and was placed on our broadcast schedule in three parts.

While at periscope depth for an extended time copying the third and last section of this long message, the Echo II unexpectedly came through the layer to periscope depth and, unbeknownst to us, visually detected our periscope just as we went deep. The Echo II commenced a series of circular baffle clearing maneuvers that lasted about two and a half hours during which time he may have gone to periscope depth. At 1:27 p.m. the Echo II increased speed to three hundred sixty-eight RPM on course 250. At 1:50 p.m. we lost contact and commenced a sprint and drift search. At 2:05 p.m. contact was held momentary. Subsequent search down his track was unsuccessful. When we realized what had happened, I was shattered! This had been my worst fear.

The maneuvers that followed, both by *Guardfish* and the Echo II, were violent and at high speed. The Soviet submarine wanted to get away and we wanted to regain contact. Holding on to an alerted contact proved to be impossible. I reported having lost contact to my operational commander and received a message directing us to terminate the operation and ordering *Guardfish* to return to Guam. The Echo II's contact message, intercepted by U.S. communication surveillance, confirmed that the Echo II had sighted me. At the time, I wondered what the Soviet skipper thought when he saw our periscope. Now, I know.

From 29 May to 6 June during our time at periscope depth receiving the broadcast, we were making brief detections of a radar operating astern of us, following us in our baffles at low speed, executing special maneuvers, although we couldn't detect anything by sonar. At 12:00 p.m., we came to periscope depth and to catch the broadcast. I made a low power periscope sweep and followed it up with a high power examination of the horizon, and there in our port quarter I saw a submarine periscope at a range of five or six cables (one-thousand-three-hundred yards) about two meters out of the water. I gave the periscope to the Executive Officer, Captain Third Rank L.V. Shaipov, and he confirmed that he saw a periscope. When I went to look again, it was gone. Sonar didn't detect anything.

Captain Berzin at K 184's periscope

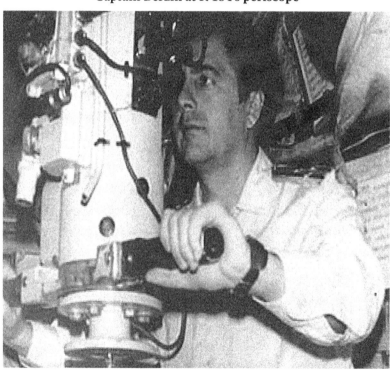

I immediately sent a message to my shore command informing them of the detection of an American submarine. We again detected a radar transmission in single sweep mode operating astern of us and assumed it was a BPS-9 radar belonging to a Permit class SSN. We dove to eighty

meters, turned about to search our baffles, speed four knots. After thirty minutes, we broke off from the American submarine, changing speed and course, using active acoustic countermeasures.

At that time we assumed that Guardfish continued to trail K 184 long after 6 June, from 7 to 9 June. Now I realize that Guardfish had lost contact and had been directed to the U.S. Naval Base in Guam. Captain Minton told me although Guardfish had received a procedure to transfer the trail on 6 June this transfer did not occur. The truth possibly remains a secret. In fact another U.S. submarine may have taken over the trail of K 184 and we periodically detected her during the period 7 to 9 June. Due to the bad hydroacoustic conditions the U.S. submarine would have had to minimize trail distance which may have allowed us to hear her. The supposition that K 184 had heard passing surface ships is untenable as we had professionals on board (same as on Guardfish) and could determine the difference between surface ships and submarines.

On 7 June, we got a message from the Soviet Pacific Fleet Command, "Maintain caution, and do not execute a trail of the American submarine." We detected a possible BPS-9 radar, bearing 172 degrees relative in a single sweep mode. By the end of the broadcast, sonar detected and held propeller sounds bearing 090 degrees relative for five minutes.

We then detected a leak of refrigerant from the circulation pump of the first circuit of the starboard reactor and I decided to vent it since the level of radioactivity and aerosols began to rise in the sixth compartment. The crew heard propeller noises from a possible submarine on the port side throughout the boat.

On 8 June our break-off maneuver from the American submarine didn't yield any results. Sonar could still detect it periodically. We sent three messages about detecting the American submarine. During the broadcast that night all the lights on the "Nakat" ESM screen were lit up ("flash" type), which gave the impression that there was a radar operating nearby; maybe one-two cables away. We immediately dove to sixty meters. The next time we came to periscope depth to catch the broadcast we again detected a BPS-9 radar. We continued our break-off course, speed, and depth while using active countermeasures.

On 9 June sonar detected a submarine bearing 150 degrees relative.

I decided to break contact with the American boat, creating two pockets of water turbulence, placing two active countermeasures between the boats and opening range by changes in course, speed and depth. I went to the navigator's stand when the junior navigator, Junior Lieutenant A.V. Konev (now a Vice Admiral and Deputy Commander of the Pacific Ocean Fleet) asked me a silly question, "Comrade Commanding Officer isn't it just like a circus ring, where our boat runs in a circle while the American boat plays trainer?" I smiled. Right then the Political Assistant, Captain Third Rank G. Ya. Antonov, called me up and asked, "Can't we just talk to the Americans?" Once the joking started, I answered back in jest, "Don your IDA-59s!"[40]

The situation in the control room was tense. You could read on people's faces the weight on their souls, but if you joked around a little bit it meant that everything would be okay. We broke off from the Americans since we couldn't detect them anymore. An Orion ASW aircraft flew in the area of the lost datum conducting a search, but we were already gone. We received an order to begin searching for an SSBN along a route measuring four hundred nautical miles. After the search we were to return to base and arrive on 19 June. The route back to base was exactly the same as the route out.

10 June. We took up our assigned position and began to search for an SSBN at 6:00 a.m. periodically we executed a baffle clearing maneuver to uncover any submarines following us. None were found.

11 June. Mid-day we came to periscope depth for the broadcast and detected a ship visually, bearing 070 degrees, range forty cables. Sonar once again didn't detect anything. Acoustic conditions for us were terrible. At 6:37 p.m. sonar heard propeller sounds. While maintaining caution, we came to periscope depth. At periscope depth we saw the stern of a fifteen thousand ton displacement ship heading away from us at a distance of about 9 cables. In this way, we determined our effective passive sonar detection range for surface contacts.

On 12 June, at 10:00 p.m., we finished our ASW search for an SSBN

---

[40] An IDA-59 is an individual isolating respiratory instrument used as life-saving equipment. It enables a submariner to breath while leaving a sunken submarine by free or buoyant ascent.

and began to transit back to base. *Forty days on deployment and there wasn't one message that came in that wasn't inflammatory in some way, and this was peacetime!*

On 13 June we got the intelligence summary:

"The ASW carrier Tripoli is enroute to Okinawa."

We would soon pass Okinawa and enter the East China Sea.

DEPARTING THE PHILIPPINE SEA

On 14 June we continue in the East China Sea.

On 15 June we came to periscope depth that night for the broadcast and nothing came to our address. The sky was clear, sea state two, visibility three miles. We shot stars and used Loran to determine our position. The crew was preparing the boat and the reports for our return to base.

ENTERING THE SEA OF JAPAN THROUGH THE KOREAN STRAITS

On 16 June at 2:00 a.m. we fixed our position near the island of Dandzo. We got a visual bearing to the lighthouse and distance to the island using the radar in single sweep mode. At 6:00 a.m., we fixed our position again and entered the Korean Straits submerged at a depth of forty meters. At 12:00 a.m. we fixed our position using Loran Alfa (four lines intersecting in one spot). On the approach to Tsushima, I wanted to confirm our position, but sonar heard the sounds of propellers, bearing 148 degrees, which escorted us for forty minutes. Sonar couldn't classify the noise. After that we again came to periscope depth to confirm our position. The weather; still, hazy, visibility twenty-thirty cables.

On 17 June we passed Ulin-Do Island in front of the surfacing point. The depth there went to two-thousand meters and more. Weather: fog, sea state two.

On 18 June there was a mass hair cutting and showering amongst the crew and everyone changes into their special clothes.

On 19 June we moored. The staff, an orchestra, and the Division Commander, Rear Admiral I.I. Verenikin, met us. A new task was put before the crew. Prepare to meet the Minister of Defense of the Soviet Union, who is coming to inspect the boat and our shore accommodations. They just took away our rest and relaxation!

And so it ended. An unforgettable twenty eight days on a historic trail. We had followed K 184 from the northernmost reaches of the Pacific Ocean to the South China Sea, an area engulfed in war. The trail would be classified for more than two and a half decades. Our job was to not lose contact with the Soviet submarine. It was a job we took very seriously, which required the dedication of the entire crew.

Despite the bombing of the Da Nang and Haiphong harbors, the Soviet navy remained uninvolved. Perhaps because they know they were being watched.

CHAPTER VII

Debrief

Rear Admiral Berzin's Analysis of the Trail

One of the amazing aspects of getting to know Rear Admiral Berzin has been an opportunity for us to exchange our perceptions and analysis of the time we spent transiting the China Sea together. The following is his current evaluation of his patrol, with the knowledge of *Guardfish's* movements. He starts with a comparison of K 184's and *Guardfish's* capabilities.

	Guardfish	K 184
Total displacement	4300 tons	5760 tons
Underwater speed	28.5 knots	23 knots
Maximum operating depth	360 meters	300 meters
Noise level *	0.1 Pascal	0.4 – 0.6 Pascal
Torpedo Tubes	4 – 533mm	4 – 533mm, 2 – 400mm
Number of torpedoes	12	16
Missiles	SUBROC	8 - P6M or 8 - P5D
Electronic Intercept	AN/WLR 2	"Nakat"
Radar	AN/BPS 9	"Albatross"
Sonar	AN/BQQ-2A AN/BQR-20 AN/BQS-6A	SHPS MG-10, MG-200, and "Plutonium"
Distance of submarine detection in favorable hydrological conditions.	75 km **	12 m ***

*   *Noise levels were defined by the experience of the author, as well as, from the U.S. and Russian press. The Echo II class submarine was so noisy it was called the "roaring cow."*

**   *Based on the sailing experience of the author, specifically from this trip, the detection range of K 184 by a submarine of the Permit class at low noise speeds was twenty-four cables (5,256 yards).*

***   *The Detection range of Guardfish at low noise speeds by K 184 was two cables (438 yards).*

Comparing Project 675 submarines and Guardfish in Table 1, you can come to the conclusion that Guardfish had an advantage over K 184 for the following:

- *Excess speed of five knots*
- *Excess depth of sixty meters*
- *Noise is less than six times*
- *Torpedoes more than four pieces*
- *The existence of weapons SUBROC, which we did not have*
- *Detection range of the sonar more than six times*
- *Guardfish also co-operated with patrol aircraft and transmitted trail information to the aircraft by the means of radio-buoy which allowed her to conduct continuous trail without the interruptions of coming to periscope depth.*
- *Patrol aircraft could use information from Guardfish to trail K 184*
- *Patrol aircraft could use their radars in single sweep mode*

All this certainly contributed to long-term tracking by Guardfish of my submarine.

Factor which contributed to the
detection of *Guardfish*

1. *Adverse hydrology in the Philippine Sea led Guardfish to shorten the tracking distance, so as to not lose contact, which in turn allowed K 184 to visually detect her at periscope depth.*
2. *Captain Minton told me that Guardfish did not use her AN/BPS-9 radar during the whole patrol.*[41]
3. *K 184 detected aircraft single pulse radar signals starting on May 27 which were mistakenly classified as AN/BPS-9 radar. Basing on the radar detections I assumed on May 27 that K 184 was being followed which was proved on June 6.*
4. *On 6 June I visually detected Guardfish at periscope depth during daylight. It could not happen if radio transmission time was ordered during the night time. Otherwise Guardfish's Captain should have come to periscope depth beyond the range of visual contact with K 184.*[42] *But what happened was what happened.*

---

[41] Rear Admiral Berzin and I compared the six times K 184 reported detecting a possible AN/BPS-9 radar with the times *Guardfish* was at periscope depth. In all but one case *Guardfish* was not at periscope depth and therefore could not have been the source of the transmissions. In addition *Guardfish* did not energize the radar at any time during the trail. We were at a loss as to the source of the transmissions. Rear Admiral Berzin suggested maybe it was the Chinese.

[42] Rear Admiral Berzin was correct that visual contact of Guardfish would not have happened if I had come to periscope depth at night or trailed at a more distant range. Because extremely noisy sonar conditions made it nearly impossible to maintain contact at night, I elected to copy our radio broadcast during daylight. Also to ensure that I would be close enough to regain contact when we went deep at the end of the broadcast, I deliberately closed the estimated contacts position. Staying at periscope depth to receive the last few minutes of the transfer message was my real mistake.

Observations on the Preparation of the Soviet Submarine Campaign

1. *Soviet Headquarters directed a transit route that had been laid on a template. Several flagship specialists saw the route. It was a flagrant violation of security and possibly compromised the mission. There wasn't any sort of cover story developed for our departure.*
2. *Our ordered return route was exactly the same as our route to the Philippine Sea, allowing any U.S. submarine to trail our submarine without much difficulty.*
3. *In preparation for the deployment all bases along our entire coast knew about the upcoming deployment of submarines. Preparations were not masked.*

In the future, Russia must build submarines which are more capable than the U.S. submarines. Example of a new high performance nuclear submarine is Cheetah K 335, which recently came into operation.

Captain of the Guardfish made a long trail of K 184 at a highly professional level.

This type of trail is potentially very dangerous because submarines cannot determine the depth of the submarine they are following. Collisions could happen and in fact they did happen during the Cold War.

During peacetime, no one country can afford to trail all the deployed ships and submarines of a potential enemy. Of course, despite the risk, trails are conducted during peacetime taking appropriate safety measures. Trails are also part of intelligence activities performed during wartime as well.

DEBRIEFING COMMANDER SUBMARINE FORCE U.S. PACIFIC AND COMMANDER-IN-CHIEF U.S. PACIFIC FLEET

Once *Guardfish* returned to Guam, I was ordered to Pearl Harbor to brief the Commander Submarine Force U.S. Pacific (COMSUBPAC), Rear Admiral P. L. Lacy Jr. and Commander-in-Chief U.S. Pacific Fleet (CINCPACFLT), Admiral B. A. Clary. I left *Guardfish* in the hands of my new Executive Officer.

Just as soon as I arrived back in Pearl Harbor I received a call from COMSUBPAC's headquarters asking me to meet informally with Rear Admiral Lacy. I was invited to come in casual clothing and meet him at the VIP cottage on Barber's Point beach. The Admiral and I sat at his kitchen table and had a beer while I described my experience. The Admiral asked quite a few questions and was very interested in the details of the trail. He was particularly interested in how his staff could have provided better support. I thanked him for setting up the special abbreviated twenty-four hour radio broadcast, approving our trailing inside the minimum trailing range, and providing us with P-3 aircraft to forward many of our messages. Because spending any time at periscope depth jeopardized our ability to maintain the trail, I did point out that his staff could have more effectively screened out parts of messages on our broadcast. Each message sent to us contained a complete list of all the other addressees and lots of extraneous verbiage all of which could have been stripped from the transmission. I remember frequently standing in the radio room door trying to will the broadcast to finish so we could get down and resume the trail.

Additionally, he asked me what I thought of the Rules of Engagement that had been relayed to us. These rules directed me to send a message if the Echo II surfaced and launched a missile. Rear Admiral Lacy and I knew each other very well. He had ridden *Guardfish* many times while we were preparing for our West Pac deployment. I felt comfortable enough to tell him my plan in the case the Echo II closed to within missile range of our surface ships on Yankee Station. I told him that if the Echo II had surfaced and launched a missile I planned to fire a

Mark 37-1 wire-guided torpedo to disable the Echo II's propulsion. After moving up on her beam, I planned to use a Mark 16 torpedo with a warhead large enough to sink the Echo II. Then I would send the message as ordered. Of course Rear Admiral P. L. Lacy Jr. could not make any comment about my plan. He just smiled. He knew me really well.

I was able to have one of my officers accompany me to Pearl Harbor to assist in the debriefing process. As a reward for outstanding performance during the trail I took Chief Warrant Officer Fred R. Heckel. Of all the Officers of the Deck, he was by far the best ship handler. Fred did an absolutely spectacular job of maintaining contact and maneuvering *Guardfish*, which of course was a continuous process requiring frequent changes of course and speed. He was especially skilled in analyzing and responding to the Echo II's baffle clearing maneuvers.

When I debriefed at CINCPACFLT headquarters, I was able to introduce Fred Heckel to Admiral Clarey as the best submarine trail Officer of the Deck in the world. I still believe that was the case. He was that good!

With the debriefings complete, Fred and I got a couple of days with our families and then flew back to Guam.

Guardfish's Trail Debriefed in Washington, D.C.

On September 11 after *Guardfish* had returned to Pearl Harbor, I was sent back to Washington, D.C. to brief senior naval and civilian staffs of many U.S. government agencies about the details of *Guardfish's* contribution to the war effort.

When I first arrived, I met with one of my old shipmates and good friend Captain George M. Vahsen, USN who was the head of the Submarine Surveillance Division in the Pentagon (OP942U). He was responsible for delivering to the White House on a daily basis the messages and updates that came from *Guardfish* during the trail, personally briefing President Nixon and the National Security Advisor, Henry Kissinger.

Captain Vahsen took me to see Vice Admiral Eugene P. "Dennis" Wilkinson, Deputy Chief of Naval Operations for Submarine Warfare, a position often referred to as the "Grey Dolphin." He was my sponsor for these briefings.[43]

Vice Admiral Wilkinson accompanied me to each of the thirteen separate briefings. He introduced me in a very folksy manner. With his hands in his pockets, he started by saying, "My name is Dennis ..... I have one of my submarine skippers here to tell you about a very interesting operation." He used this ploy to lull the attendees into thinking I would be fresh blood, not being aware of the significance of their questions. When a politically sensitive question was thrown at me he would show up like magic at my side saying, "I'll take that." I was fortunate to have him backing me up because I had little or no knowledge about the infighting between the various agencies.

During that visit he also told me what had taken place in Washington, D.C. during my trail. It was extremely gratifying to me. I talked to so many senior officers during the briefings that I began to pay little attention to Admirals and Generals that had fewer than three stars. My briefings lasted for two tiring days and included the Chairman of the Joint Chiefs of Staff, the Assistant Secretary of Defense (Intelligence), the Deputy Director of Defense Research and Engineering, the Deputy Director of the CIA, representatives from Office of the Chief of Naval Operations, Flag Officers from the Naval Material Command, and countless senior staffers.

Of all the briefings I gave, the most interesting to me was to George Vahsen's staff at OP942U, the group responsible for monitoring submarine surveillance patrols. They processed and analyzed information from all submarine surveillance patrol and special operation reports. It turned out that most of OP942U's staff were young women who were very, very knowledgeable about submarines operations. They asked the

---

[43] Eugene P. "Dennis" Wilkinson was a U.S. Naval officer selected for three historic command assignments. The first, in 1954, when Admiral Rickover selected him as the first Commanding Officer of the USS *Nautilus* (SSN 571) the world's first nuclear submarine. The second in 1961, when Admiral Rickover again selected him to serve as the first Commanding Officer of the USS *Long Beach* (CGN 9), America's first nuclear surface ship. The third was in 1980 when he was chosen to be the first President and CEO of the Institute for Nuclear Power Operations (INPO) from which he retired in 1984.

most intelligent questions of any audience I'd briefed and had a better appreciation of what was going on during our trail than any of the senior officers I'd talked to. It was a fascinating discussion.

Finally, I met with Admiral Rickover in his private office. The Admiral, as I expected, was most interested in how the reactor plant had performed. I could honestly say that we had no problems.

CHAPTER VIII

The Remainder of the Six Month Deployment

Guardfish Returns to Guam for Upkeep

We commenced the four day transit to Guam on June 6th, as directed. On the way we finally had a chance to do some housekeeping. As I described before we had been stowing all of our garbage on board instead of using the garbage ejector. The dry garbage was compacted and stowed in the number one auxiliary trim tank. The wet garbage was stowed in the freeze box almost filling it with the worst smelly stuff you can imagine. The crew called the frozen garbage trash-sickles. Now as we transited to Guam for some much needed rest and recreation we had the distasteful task of getting rid of all that trash. We had the choice of surfacing and dumping the weighted trash overboard or return to Guam and use most of a day dumping trash in containers on the pier and cleaning up the boat instead of liberty and relaxation. There was no real choice! We surfaced!

During a normal deployment to the Western Pacific, a nuclear submarine would conduct a sixty day submerged special operation and then have a three week or more inport period for normal repairs and rest and relaxation, followed by another sixty days submerged special operation. When *Guardfish* returned to Guam on June 10 the crew had been underway submerged for one hundred twenty-three days broken only by an eight day rapid refit and replenishment. Despite conducting two demanding special operations, including the unprecedented and exhausting twenty-eight day

Echo II trail, *Guardfish's* morale was sky high. The officers and crew were justifiably proud of what they had accomplished.

Interestingly, despite the secrecy and covertness of the trail, when I returned to Guam I was given a copy of the May 28 *Stars and Stripes Military Newspaper* containing the following article

"SOVIET MISSILE SUBS OFF VIET, DOD SAYS

Washington (UPI) — Four Soviet nuclear-powered submarines carrying surface-to-surface missiles have been holding a position off the Vietnamese coast in the South China Sea for several days, Defense Department sources said Friday. Sources said the Soviet Union might use these subs and eight other Soviet warships, which took up a position about two hundred miles off the coast of Vietnam a few days earlier, for a show of force once the Moscow summit conference ends.

For the past several days, sources said, the submarines have been between the Paracel Islands and the Philippines, well out of range of the U.S. warships patrolling in the Tonkin Gulf off North Vietnam's seven mined ports.

All four submarines belong to the "E-class" and carry both torpedoes and surface-to-surface Shaddock missiles with a nominal range of two hundred nautical miles One of them has six missile launchers and the other three eight missiles apiece. Sources said they were not particularly concerned about the presence of the other eight ships, which include a guided missile cruiser, five destroyers, and an oil tanker because they could keep track of these forces. As a precaution the State Department dispatched the anti-submarine aircraft carrier, USS *Ticonderoga* to Southeastern Asia to provide additional anti-submarine protection."

I still do not know what to make of it. It appears to me that the DOD had leaked this information to influence the Soviets to withdraw their submarines and warships from the South China Sea. We knew on *Guardfish* the Soviet submarines had been called back on May 24.

GUARDFISH CONTINUES HER WESTPAC DEPLOYMENT

Guardfish's crew would not return to Pearl Harbor and be reunited with their families and friends for another two months.

Our next port of call was Yokosuka, Japan, where I met with the Commander Submarine Flotilla Seven and took advantage of the situation to make a special request. Because of the nature of our operation, we were reporting directly to Commander Seventh Fleet, which meant I could request that my award recommendations go through Seventh Fleet instead of the typical administrative chain of command. This was unusual, but it had one important benefit. Awards processed through my administrative chain of command could take months to return. Recommendations to Seventh Fleet were back within a week if the administrative chain of command didn't object in writing. The key benefit was that almost all of the awards would be returned and could be presented before any of my shipmates were transferred through normal rotation to new duty stations. Delaying awards really dilutes the impact of the award and was detrimental to morale. To my surprise my request was granted and the Executive Officer and I quickly put together the awards package and sent it off. In light of the Navy's current practice of handing out more and more medals I probably should have recommended more and higher levels of awards, but in 1972 the awards package we submitted was considered pushing the limit.

For all the seriousness of our mission, submariners always find a way to keep things interesting. For instance, while we were in Yokosuka, Japan, I became aware of a stowaway on board *Guardfish*. When we left Guam, my crew had hidden a little duckling on board. His name was Spot and his shipmates worked hard at cleaning up after him (thus his name) and moving him from one compartment to another to keep me from seeing him. Apparently this was difficult when I was conducting a below decks inspection. While in port I had a habit of taking a walk on the pier in the evening. On one such occasion, I got to chat with one of my sonarmen as we watched a young duckling swimming in a puddle on the pier. Much to my surprise, I discovered that this duckling was my stowaway! Unfortunately Spot was unable to continue the deployment as he met with a fatal accident while on liberty in town. His handler fell off his bar stool onto the duck in his jacket pocket.

When we arrived in Hong Kong several weeks later most of the awards were waiting for us. Two members of my crew were scheduled for transfer at our next port of call, Subic Bay, Philippines. Getting the awards back so quickly meant we could present the awards prior to their departure.

On our way to Subic Bay from Hong Kong we were able to pass through a corner of the Vietnam War Zone where I reenlisted seven of the *Guardfish* crew. Reenlisting in a war zone allowed them to receive their reenlistment bonuses tax free. Even without counting these seven reenlistments *Guardfish* was runner up for the 1972 Pacific Submarine Force Golden Anchor Award for the highest reenlistment rate.

This picture shows me awarding Warrant Officer Fred Heckle the Meritorious Service Medal. I conducted this ceremony on the pier in Subic Bay.

This picture shows me awarding Machinist Mate Second Class Tomas E. Cosgrove the Navy Achievement Medal.

The Executive Officer, Lieutenant Commander Larry Vogt, also left *Guardfish* in Subic Bay. He was a fine officer and I had relied heavily on his knowledge and experience. I really hated to see him go. He and I were the only members of the crew that had to wait for our awards so I was unable to present his award prior to his departure. However, the officers and crew presented the XO with the farewell monkey pod plaque in recognition of our respect for his professional and dedicated service shown below.

RETURNING TO OUR HOME PORT

On August 17, we finally returned to Pearl Harbor and were reunited with our families and friends. The crew had been away from their home port for one hundred and ninety-one days. This was a traditional homecoming with the families on the pier and the submarine decked out with a homecoming lei. The purple lei was made by the wives and carried out to us by a torpedo retriever as we started in the channel. The lei is the almost indistinguishable fuzzy dark thing hanging around the front of the sail. As with all Navy homecomings, there were lots of happy faces on board and on the pier.

AWARDS CEREMONY

On September 8, after a well-deserved down period for the crew to reconnect with their families, *Guardfish* had an awards ceremony on the pier at Submarine Base Pearl Harbor. Commander Submarine Squadron Seven, Captain Robert W. Chewning USN, presided at the ceremony. The following are some of the pictures of that ceremony. [44]

---

[44] A complete list of awards is contained in Appendix H.

Guardfish's sail flanked by the officers and chief petty officers to the left and rest of the crew to the right

Commander Submarine Squadron Seven, Captain Robert W. Chewning USN, inspecting the crew.

FROM OPPOSITE SIDES OF THE PERISCOPE

Captain Robert W. Chewning USN awarding Navy
Commendation Medals to (Left to right) LT R. C. Woodward
USN, LTJG H. A. Williams USN, LT E. D. Bartel USN, STC
(SS) W. L. Treese USN, and ST1 (SS) H. K. Wilson USN.

Captain Robert W. Chewning USN awarding Navy Achievement Medals to MM2 (SS) T. R. Lindberg USN and LCDR R. L. Graham USN two of the five Navy Achievement Medals awarded for this operation.

From Opposite Sides of the Periscope

Captain Robert W. Chewning USN awarding COMSEVENTHFLT Commendations (Left to right) to LTJG G. R. Whaley USN, LT A. J. Sisk USN, LTJG L. G. Lewis USN, LTJG M. Kovar USN, RMC (SS) A. O'Meally USN, MMC (SS) J.C. Seifert USN, IC1 (SS) R.C. Crespin USN, QM1 (SS) (Dv) C.F. Williams USN, and YN2 (SS) R.W. Sandberg USN.

Captain Robert W. Chewning USN awarding some of the eighteen COMSUBPAC Commendations.

In July 1972 the USS *Guardfish* received her third consecutive yearly Battle Efficiency Award and her fourth consecutive Torpedo Performance Award for Submarine Division Seventy-Two.

Soon after my return I, unfortunately, encountered some medical problems that eventually required extended hospitalization. Because of this, Commander B. G. Balderson, Commander Submarine Division Seventy-Two, assumed command of *Guardfish* on December 15, 1972, without the usual pomp and circumstances of the traditional naval ceremony. It was really hard for me to leave *Guardfish* and my crew in this manner.

After several trying months in two different hospitals I was returned to duty and took command of the oldest (first) Polaris submarine, USS *George Washington* (SSBN 598) (Gold).

On March 13, 1973, there occurred one of the most unusual changes of command in the history of the U.S. Submarine Force. In contrast with the administrative process by which Commander Balderson had taken command of *Guardfish*, Commander W.S. Rich, a good friend and Naval Academy classmate, had a formal change of command with a band and all the regular pomp. Traditionally, the outgoing Commanding Officer speaks, but since I was underway on the *George Washington*, I wrote some remarks for Commander Balderson to read for me. My wife, Marilyn, and our kids attended the ceremony as part of the official party along with Commander Balderson's and Commander Rich's families. It was kind of a three ring circus. Captain Chewning presided and was the principal speaker. He included remarks to Commander Balderson, Commander Rich, and to me. One comment apparently got quite a laugh. He said, "I would also report that the drive and energy which helped make him (Commander Minton) standout as a Commanding Officer made him an equally bad hospital patient." Because I never received a letter of detachment from *Guardfish* I have always contended that I was in command of two nuclear submarines at the same time. On July 14, 1973, I was honored to attend the ceremony presenting *Guardfish* with a Navy Unit Commendation for our patrol. My only regret was that the crew did not get the Presidential Unit Commendation that had been recommended and which they truly deserved.

The citation for the Navy Unit Commendation read in part:

> "For exceptionally meritorious service during the spring of 1972 while conducting operations as a unit of the United States Pacific Fleet the USS *Guardfish* (SSN 612) completed three extraordinarily demanding operations of great value and lasting significance to the Government of the United States."

At that same ceremony my old crew gave me a beautiful plaque mounted on a carved tropical wood backing. It is displayed with honor in my family room.

In this photo MMC (SS) Napoleon G. Bragado, *Guardfish's* Chief of the Boat, presented the plaque to me.

On January 11, 1974, I was awarded the Distinguished Service Medal. It was presented to me by Vice Admiral St. George, Deputy Commander in Chief of the U.S. Pacific Fleet. In attendance were Admiral Clarey USN (Ret.), Rear Admiral McMullen COMSUBPAC, Rear Admiral P. L. Lacy Jr. USN (Ret.), the crew of my new command

USS *George Washington* (SSBN 598) (Gold), my wife and kids, and my parents who made a special trip from Ohio for this occasion.

In this photo I am shaking hands with Vice Admiral St. George, Deputy Commander in Chief U.S. Pacific Fleet, and my wife, Marilyn, looked on while I received the Distinguished Service Medal (the Navy's highest non-combat award).

On board a submarine there exists a very close bond between all the men. Everyone knows each member of the crew, you know their foibles, you know their strengths, and you respect their professionalism. I had a very very strong attachment to my officers and crew. In fact I considered them not as officers and crew, but as shipmates. We were shipmates and we had been part of a great adventure. It was my privilege to have sailed with them in *Guardfish*.

CHAPTER IX

КАРЬЕРА ПОСЛЕ ТРЕЙЛ

(Careers after the Trail)

After World War II, the work on designing and building nuclear powered submarines began in the United States, Britain, France, and the USSR. The possibility of a Cold War confrontation between the USSR and the countries belonging to NATO seemed to be growing with each passing year.

The first nuclear powered submarines that came into operation were the U.S. Navy's USS *Nautilus* (SSN 571), in January 1955, followed by the Soviet Navy's SSGN K 3 (November class submarine) in January 1959.[45] Almost immediately and to this day nuclear powered submarines have been used to explore the Arctic Ocean. The first submarines to reach the North Pole were the *Nautilus* in 1958 and the Soviet K 3 in 1962. Later, the U.S. and the USSR systematically used, and continue to use, the Arctic for the following tasks:

1. Patrolling nuclear submarines with ballistic missiles with readiness to strike on the orders from their Higher Commands.

---

[45] Soviet submarines of the first generation didn't have a name. Later submarines were given both numbers and names. So the Soviet submarines in this book are only referred to by number.

First U.S. ballistic missile submarines (SSBNs) and then the Soviet guided missile submarines (SSGNs) were deployed.

2. Providing protection for SSBNs and the SSGNs using the support of nuclear attack submarines (SSNs).

3. Search for and trailing SSBNs and SSGNs using SSNs during the peacetime in readiness to destroy their opponents in the event of a war.

4. In the USSR (and now Russia), there is still a task of the relocation of certain classes of nuclear submarines from the Northern Fleet to the Pacific Fleet, and vice versa, in order to strengthen the respective groups of submarines.[46]

Tasks 1 through 3 could be accomplished all year-round, but relocation (task 4) was feasible only during a short period, from the end of August to early September. At other times the ice situation made it too complex and difficult. Ice prevented nuclear submarines from surfacing at the one hundred meter curve in the Chukchi Sea and the Bering Sea; at the same time, shallow depths in these areas do not allow a submarine to pass under the ice submerged.

SSGN K 43 made the transit together with a nuclear ballistic submarine (SSBN). The director of the campaign, Vice Admiral L.A. Matushkin, was embarked on that SSBN.

In 1979, the headquarters of the Pacific Fleet planned two events in the Chukchi Sea. First, the meeting of nuclear submarine K 320, which was to make the transit from the Northern Fleet to the Pacific Fleet; and, second, a historic first for the Pacific Fleet, the voyage of K 212 in the Chukchi Sea beneath the ice to 76 degrees north latitude, two hundred-forty miles south of the North Pole. It was to be a fearsome patrol.

Swimming under the ice has a number of special features. In case of fire, flooding, or radiation hazards a submarine cannot just float to the surface, due to the ice over its hull; instead it must look for surfacing polynya, a break in the ice, either natural or made by an icebreaker.

---

[46] Appendix E contains a table showing the relocation of nuclear submarines from the Soviet Northern Fleet to the Pacific Fleet from 1963 – 1968 during Admiral Berzin's command.

If it takes more than several minutes or even seconds to find a polynya the submarine may be lost. There is a good reason why commanders receive the honorary title of "Hero of the Soviet Union" for the transfer of a submarine from the Barents Sea to the Pacific Ocean under the ice of the Arctic Ocean and. the rest of the crew receives awards, medals, valuable gifts, and citations: Submerged operations under the ice are always associated with some risk.

You could say it was a fee for fear. Some of the Division Officers considered Berzin to be lucky. Before a voyage or any other new task he would be very nervous and even scared, he would ask himself the question "Can I handle this?" This excitement and sense of responsibility for his submarine crew forced him to carefully prepare himself and take steps to prepare the crew and equipment for the assignment. When it was time to start a patrol the fear and uncertainty would disappear.

Many of the submarine officers and crew were afraid of under ice operations because there was so little margin for error. Fear is a dangerous thing because people take unreasonable actions often endangering their shipmates. While taking commander's classes in Leningrad, Berzin often met with one of the old submariners, a war veteran, who told him many stories about the past. One such story happened in May 1943. Submarine U 303 left for a war patrol and had to go through the Gulf of Finland to reach the Baltic Sea. Between Tallinn and Porkala the Germans had established an anti-submarine network containing many bottom and conventional mines in two rows. Anti-submarine ships patrolled along the network. Trying to break through the line, the submarine came across the network twice, and every attempt to break through or find a passage was unsuccessful.

When the battery capacity dropped to the lower limit the submarine had to surface to charge the battery. Near the end of the charge the Commanding Officer discovered German anti-submarine boats had detected them, and the submarine had to dive. They evaded the boats by lying on the bottom. It was peaceful on board, and the Commanding Officer decided to rest in his cabin, leaving a Navigator in charge in the adjacent control room.

In about thirty minutes sonar heard the noise of the antisubmarine boat's propellers. Chief Officer Galkin suggested to the Navigator that he report the contact to the Commanding Officer. Long ago at the base, Galkin had begun to suffer from a fear that his submarine would be killed by mines or depth bombs. As soon as the Navigator left, Galkin acted on this fear. He jammed the door of the control room and radio room where the radio operator and sonar operators were located so nobody could get to him. He turned off the power to all devices and blew the main ballast tanks. The submarine surfaced. Galkin pushed open the upper conning tower hatch, stuck a white rag on the bridge, went on the deck, and walked to the stern where he waved his hand, beckoning the German boats.

The gunner and a sonarman on duty heard the main ballast tanks blow and moved to investigate. They broke open the jammed door and ran into the adjacent compartment. This allowed the Commanding Officer to climb to the bridge where he saw approaching German boats and Galkin on the stern. The Captain ordered an emergency dive and again the submarine evaded the German boats and lay on the bottom. The Germans dropped about two hundred depth bombs near the submarine but were not able to destroy it. The Germans pulled Galkin out of the water, and he subsequently started to cooperate with them. In the history of the fleet there are a sufficient number of examples where a person under the fear of dying, or as a result of panic actions caused the death of other people.

In 1974, Alfred Berzin had been relieved as Command Officer of K 184 and placed at the disposal of the main Navy Commander in Leningrad. In September 1976, he was reassigned as the Chief of Staff of the 26th Submarine Division, and later as Deputy Commander of the 10th Submarine Division in the Pacific Fleet. In 1979, he was the Commander of the 10th Submarine Division, part of the Soviet Fleet which operated under the ice.

As the Captain of K 212 prepared for his historic patrol, Berzin received a radio message which ordered the submarine to transit submerged toward the base under the ice for several hours. On arrival at the base they were to surface at the center of a polynya which was made by an icebreaker. The polynya size was to be five by ten miles.

Berzin's campaign staff was headed by Captain First Rank N.V. Anokhin, who was on the icebreaker *Ivan Susanin*. The preparation of nuclear submarine Charlie class K 212 for the campaign included the following:

- Provisioning to 100 percent parts and consumables
- Loading two torpedoes, which could be deployed to explode beneath the ice to create an opening for ascent in case of emergency
- Working out a full course of training
- Exploring and studying the transit route
- Introduction of K 212 personnel to my divisional headquarters and Pacific Fleet procedures

Studying navigational and hydrological information led to the following conclusions about expected ice conditions: The two-year polar ice thickness was not less than two meters and the elevation of the surface hummocks had been smoothed out. The Arctic pack (or multi-year ice) thickness was of two and one half meters or greater, the surface was hilly, and the ice fractures were colored blue. In some areas of the Arctic there was very peculiar drifting ice, ice islands, with a thickness of seventy to eighty meters, and their elevation above sea level reached twelve meters.

In preparation for the campaign Berzin and his team also studied the experience that was gained during the transfer of other nuclear submarines from the Northern Fleet to the Pacific Fleet.

Charlie class submarine like K 212 and K 320

Submarine deployment of K 212 consisted of the following steps:

1. Transit to the Chukchi Sea
2. Rendezvous with K 320
3. Submerged training under the ice
4. Two days submerged operation under the ice at 76 degrees north latitude
5. Return to the base

TRANSIT TO THE CHUKCHI SEA

On Sunday, August 26 at 5:00 a.m., the Soviet submarine SSGN K 212 (Charlie 1 class) moved away from the pier. All day they operated on the surface at a speed of four knots to the diving point. The location was planned by Pacific Fleet headquarters so that K 212 could act as a decoy and the SSBN returning from a patrol could pass safely undetected by U.S. anti-submarine forces.

On Monday, August 27, three times during the day they came to periscope depth to receive radio communication from the base and to fix our position. During each rise to periscope depth they discovered that a U.S. Orion anti-submarine aircraft was searching in their area, indicating that K 212 was being tracked, and their passing the SSBN on August 26 had not been wasted. The U.S. had turned off their drift station Loran Charlie navigational aid, which created some difficulties for the submarine to determine its location.

On Tuesday, August 28, K 212 passed the islands of Bering and Copper on the left, and the Attu Island on the right. They were running at a speed of fifteen knots according to the operation plan. At this speed, they clearly would be detected by the U.S. fixed sonar system, SOSUS.

On Wednesday, August 29, each time they came to periscope depth for a radio communication broadcast from the base, they observed fog clouds at ten points, which completely excluded the possibility of fixing their location through celestial navigation.

On Thursday, August 30, they surfaced when the depth reduced to one hundred meter depth (three hundred thirty-five feet), as the sea became shallower, they surfaced. All further movement would be on the surface until they reached the Chukchi Sea. They were on their way to meet with the sea-going tug MB 147 and continued movement north.

On Friday, August 31, K 212 passed Providence Bay; the coast could barely be seen[47]. Tomorrow they would pass Cape Dezhnev.

On Saturday, September 1, K 212 passed through the Bering Straits. Through the periscope they could see Dezhnev[48] monument, on the most eastern coast of Russia.

On Sunday, September 2, K 212 has entered the Chukchi Sea. On

---

[47] Providence Bay is a convenient deep water bay that has long attracted seafarers. For almost two hundred years it was nameless. This romantic bay was named by the English seamen on the sailing ship *Plover*, commanded by Thomas Moore. In 1848 – 1849, years of harsh winters. *Plover's* crew suffered distress and were compelled to winter over there. To celebrate a successful winter, Captain Moore called this the happiest place, Bay St. Providence.

[48] Cape Dezhnev was first passed in 1648, by an expedition of explorers from the Kolyma River, led by the Cossack Semyon Dezhnev and merchant Fedot Alexeyev.

the horizon the clouds form a false impression of earth, ice, and fantastic shapes. Tomorrow they will get close to the islands of Wrangel and Herald. The traces of an 18th century Chukchi village were found on the western shore of the island near Cape Thomas. It was first shown on maps (and fairly accurately) by the Chukchi hydrographer Wrangel in 1823. The strait between Wrangel Island and the mainland was named after him. Herald Island is located thirty miles east of Wrangel Island was discovered in 1849 by the British ship *Herald*, in whose honor it was named.

On Monday, September 3, K 212 passed Herald Island and started to meet individual ice floes, which looked like small ships. Flaws in the ice were blue. From the camp staff they received information about the position to meet SSGN K 320 and the location of the boundary of ice.

On Tuesday, September 4, using radar they had found the detachment of support ships at the ice edge and established radio contact with the icebreaker *Ivan Susanin*. In thirty minutes they sighted the team: at anchor was the GTRI *Anadyr*, in the drift ice the icebreaker *Litke*, and the icebreaker *Ivan Susanin* in the ice. Over the radio, Berzin contacted the head of the formation staff Captain First Rank N.V. Anokhin to clarify the situation. The right shaft of icebreaker *Litke* was broken. Diving operations were required so as not to lose the screw. On September 5, at 10:00 p.m., four sonar beacons were put up to assist K 320 in surfacing. After discussion, it was decided to move K 212 to the very edge of the ice. Some of the ice was loose, broken up; some was in large blocks. On the ice were walruses and polar bears, which were not afraid of people or ships.

RENDEZVOUS WITH K 320

On Wednesday, September 5, K 212 was located twenty miles south of the ice-breaker *Ivan Susanin* waiting for K 320 to surface. The U.S. anti-submarine aircraft Orion flew over and started his overflights of our ships at a low altitude. The icebreaker *Ivan Susanin* reported that nuclear submarine K 320 emerged at the surface and under the guidance of MB 147 started to move towards us. A few minutes later we sighted them, we slowed down so we could communicate. We made radio contact and Berzin congratulated the crew on the successful completion of their patrol. The senior officer aboard, Rear Admiral E.D. Chernov, a Hero of the Soviet Union, reported that they were all right. They had surfaced in a polynya, two hundred miles from the edge of the ice. The ice in the polynya was twenty centimeters thick. The thickness of the ice edge was five to seven meters. Explosive devices, which were carried by the icebreaker *Ivan Susanin*, had been heard from a distance of forty-four miles and the signals of the sonar beacons were detected from twenty miles away. We wished them "Godspeed" and K 320 started to move with MB 147 toward the base.

K 212 requested permission from the Commander of the Pacific Fleet to operate under the ice for training. While waiting for an answer, they prepared to dive. They had adapted air pressure for the middle group of main ballast tanks to control the process of emerging vertically to the surface without motion in a polynya.

SUBMERGED TRAINING UNDER THE ICE

They received their answer from the Operational Duty Officer, "Start a training cruise from 9:00 p.m. on September 5." Berzin discussed all necessary questions with Captain First Rank N.V. Anokhin, wished each other all good things and went under the water towards the northern sonar beacon. According to sonar trace and their mine-sweeping sonar, the depth of the ice appeared to be fifty meters. At a speed of seven knots they noted certain parts of the ice were only ten meters thick. They had to increase their depth to sixty meters. It was night; they went under the ice, everything calmed down, and life went on as usual.

On Thursday, September 6, since submerging K 212 constantly heard the explosions from the icebreaker *Ivan Susanin*. At 2:00 a.m. they turned in the opposite direction. Berzin detected sonar beacons MO 1 and 2 and determined that they were sixteen miles from the *Ivan Susanin*. He planned his surfacing point to be three miles aft of the *Ivan Susanin*. At the appointed time they surfaced and measured the distance by radar to the ice-breaker – it was three miles. They reported to the Pacific Fleet Commander that they had completed the training cruise and requested permission for an additional two-day cruise under the ice. After lunch the weather had deteriorated; the wind increased to fifteen meters/second, the sea state was five, and clouds were ten points. They went to the area of sonar beacon MO 4 and the icebreaker *Ivan Susanin* and then went into the ice. At 1:59 p.m. the reactor emergency alarm sounded due to operator error. This was easily fixed and the main power plant continued to work normally. Despite the bad weather, a U.S. Orion anti-submarine aircraft flew over again and began methodically flying over for three hours. In the evening they received a radio message from the Fleet Commander; he gave K 212 permission to cruise under the ice from 2:00 a.m. on September 7 to 2:00 a.m. on September 9. The sea state was at five, it was raining, and the wind was seventeen meters/second (thirty-eight miles per hour).

TWO DAY SUBMERGED OPERATION UNDER THE ICE AT LATITUDE 76 DEGREES NORTH

On Friday, September 7, Berzin sent a radio message to the Pacific Fleet Commander that he was commencing the cruise and submerged to a depth of forty meters, then fifty, seventy, and finally to one hundred meters. They were under the ice. At the periscope there was a continuous watch, one could hear; "Dark, dark, light." When they heard a report of "light" it meant that there was clear water or a thin young ice layer between the ice floes. They were moving farther and farther to the north; above, the ice was two to seven meters thick. When they reached latitude 76 north, they began patrolling in the area designated number one looking for a polynya to surface in so they could send a status report to the Soviet Pacific Fleet Commander.

On Saturday, September 8, the Orion followed their course, trying to find the ship. They continued to look for a polynya. Finally, they discovered one with a length of about nine cables.[49] Taking into consideration the current, K 212 rose to the location and without forward

---

[49] Soviet Navy frequently uses cables to measure short distances. One cable is seven hundred twenty-five feet or two hundred twenty yards in the U. S. Navy.

movement we began to slowly rise toward periscope depth. When they received a report from the periscope, "no ice," they lowered the periscope, sent some bubbles to the middle group of the main ballast tanks, and emerged another five meters. Once on the surface they raised the periscope. It was sunny, blue sky, with white ice all around, and the submarine was in the middle of the ice. The ice around the polynya had been broken. The ice pieces were one and one half to two meters thick, and between them there was thin ice from one to ten centimeters thick. Some of the crew went up to the bridge; all around was quiet, white silence. A walrus could be seen near the deck; he was looking at the men with interest, and then he dove under the boat and, floated on the other side, where he continued his observations. At 1:20 p.m. K 212 submerged and continued toward the escort ships.

These are some of the walrus sighted in the Arctic.

On Sunday, September 9, K 212 surfaced at the designated location at 2:00 a.m.

Return to the Base

A convoy of ships and K 212 formed a line ahead and began the transit towards the base. Later Berzin transferred to the icebreaker *Ivan Susanin*. In the Bering Sea, K 212 surfaced and proceeded to their assigned patrol area; they would not return to their base until a month later. The convoy arrived in Petropavlovsk Kamchatka on September 17. New trips were waiting for them, as well as new tasks and practical weapons firing.

The Fleet's usual procedure of, "Punish the innocent and reward the uninvolved" was not applied in this case. K 212 was simply forgotten. [50]

The picture below is of Captain First Rank Alfred Berzin in the wardroom of the K 204 while embarked as the Senior Officer in 1980. He was then the Commander of Soviet Submarine 10th Division. Note the classic samovar, the bread, and the tea, which was the non-alcoholic drink of choice aboard Soviet ships.

---

[50] Berzin is saying the usual awards and recognition for dangerous under ice operations were not awarded and the senior staff just ignored the whole operation.

Alfred Berzin received the military rank Rear Admiral after being a Commander of the 10th Division of Pacific Fleet for only five years, a rare exception in the personnel policy of the Soviet Navy at that time.

From 1982 to 1988, he returned to Leningrad as head of the Department of Navy Tactics, 6th Higher Special Officer Class for the Soviet Navy Fleet.

In 1988, he was discharged from naval service and retired in Leningrad.

From 1999 to 2007, he worked at a closed joint-stock company "The Central Company of Financial-Industrial Group, Marine Technology" as an Assistant Production General Director.

Rear Admiral Berzin is currently fully retired and lives in St. Petersburg.

MINTON'S CAREER AFTER THE TRAIL

In March 1973, I took command of USS *George Washington* (Gold) (SSBN 598) during her submerged transit from Charleston, South Carolina, to the Panama Canal and on into the Pacific. *George Washington* was then based in Guam, while our families and off crew facilities remained in Hawaii. The *Washington* had been a troubled ship in the Atlantic. She was the oldest Polaris submarine and had not been well cared for. She had twice failed the ORSE and had numerous long standing material problems. For medical reasons, the previous Commanding Officer, Commander David Fields, had been relieved by an interim Commanding Officer, Commander Bud Foster. When I got to the *Washington* I realized why they had given me this assignment. In my case, the detailer had bypassed a number of requirements for command of a SSBN. I had not attended the prerequisite navigational and weapons schools but apparently made up for it by my extensive experience and reputation for caring for engineering plants. After I relieved Bud Foster during the submerged transit to the Panama Canal, I started to make a list of the most pressing and significant engineering issues. I titled it "Impossible Problems" because success- fully addressing these issues had eluded staff and crew for several years. As a result of nagging material problems, no one in the crew had ever experienced the *Washington* getting underway on time. Just prior to getting underway for my first patrol, while I was escorting the Squadron Commander through the boat, we had a reactor scram and at the same time discovered a significant leak from a main steam valve flange. Despite these problems I ordered the *Washington* to get underway on time, if necessary on the diesel. I announced to a meeting of officers in the wardroom that, "We are leaving on time; even if I had to push the boat away from the tender myself."

They got the word, and we left Guam for patrol on time operating on the reactor using a single steam loop until we could repair the steam leak. From that time on we were never late meeting our schedule. I made three Polaris patrols in *George Washington* and on each patrol I was able to cross off problems on my "Impossible Problems" list until it was complete. The Engineer Officer, Lieutenant Commander Michael Oliver, had been the Engineering Department Head during the two ORSE failures and was expecting to leave George *Washington* prior to the next exam. Much to his surprise and concern, I didn't allow him to leave. I told him he had to "win one" before he was transferred, and I would help him. We received an Above Average grade on the next ORSE, which was excellent for a submarine of *Washington's* age. Mike went to his next assignment a winner. Subsequently he was assigned his own submarine command.

The last patrol was classified as a flex-operation. As such we did not occupy a usual patrol area but were assigned a series of training operations, including a port visit in Pearl Harbor. In case of an increase in DEFCON we were fully ready to move to a Polaris patrol area and assume our deterrent posture. This type of patrol allowed us to provide services to U.S. anti-submarine forces, and helped train our junior officers with multiple dives and surfaces, plus using the radio to coordinate exercises.

Prior to our port visit in Hawaii, we conducted a series of tests of SSBN vulnerability to being trailed by Soviet submarines while exiting a port. I figured that the tests were rigged since *George Washington* was the oldest SSBN and a member of an inherently loud SSBN class. Each test was started with *George Washington* on the surface simulating a submarine exiting an imaginary port on the west coast of Oahu,

Hawaii. We were opposed by the USS *Pogy* (SSN 647), a top of the line 637 class attack submarine. The *Pogy* remained submerged patrolling off of the coast. Once the test started I would submerge the *George Washington* and commence an evasive maneuver. As a result of my experience on *Guardfish* I knew that immediately conducting baffle clearing maneuvers, which had become a common practice used by SSBN commanding officers, only resulted in remaining at or near the submerging datum, giving the *Pogy* a real advantage.

My tactic instead was to turn parallel to the coastline one way or the other, rig for ultra-quiet, and open out quickly away from the datum at ever increasing speeds. The surf noise to the east aided in masking *Washington's* movements. Once I felt that I had lost *Pogy*, I turned west to open the coast. At the end of each test I was free, clear, and undetected.

After three of these frustrating tests the Commanding Officer of *Pogy* decided to use active sonar to gain and hold contact; however echo-ranging into the shallow coast was no better, and it gave us the advantage of having a bearing to our opponent. By comparing sound bouncing off the bottom to the sound coming to us in a direct path we also had a continuous and accurate range. At the end of the last of five test runs we joined up with *Pogy*, and they initiating an underwater telephone (UQC) range check. A range check is started by one submarine counting down from five and then starting a stopwatch at a silent zero, the last transmission. The receiving submarine transmits, "Mark" when they heard countdown completed. Usually the initiating submarine would calculate the range using the speed of sound in the water and, the time difference, and then transmit the range to the other submarine. Because I already had the range, I transmitted the actual range along with the "mark". I understand the *Pogy's* Commanding Officer was furious at his submarine's inability to track *George Washington* and at my showing off by giving him the range when I was not expected to have it. Several days later *George Washington* returned to port signaling her clean sweep by flying a broom from her mast.

George Washington subsequently received the Squadron Fifteen Battle Efficiency "E" which reflected our crew's unofficial motto "Not getting older, just getting better."

I was relieved from *George Washington* on June 28, 1975, and I assigned for two years as the Readiness Office for Squadron Three in San Diego, California. My primary duty was to train and prepare the attack submarines in our squadron for their annual Operational Reactor Safeguards Examination (ORSE). During this tour I was promoted to Captain. It turned out that I spent as much time at sea during this tour as I had on *George Washington*.

The last three years of my naval career, I was assigned as the Commander Submarine Forces Pacific (COMSUBPAC), Commander Naval Air Forces Pacific (COMNAVAIRPAC), and Commander Naval U.S. Surface Forces Pacific (COMSURFPAC) representative for nuclear overhauls at the Naval Shipyard Bremerton, Washington. This job was very interesting in that I was frequently battling the Shipyard Commander along with the Naval Reactors Representative to keep the overhauls on time. The shipyard would not acknowledge that they were way behind in their overhauls. Getting them to provide a realistic schedule of when a ship would be ready to leave the yard was impossible. For example, when the USS Enterprise (CVN 65) entered the shipyard the overhaul was scheduled for fifteen months, but by the time work was started it had been rescheduled for eighteen months. I had taken this schedule and where the shipyard had scheduled reactor testing of many of their eight reactors in parallel; I rearranged the testing in series. I knew that the shipyard had never tested more than one reactor plant at any time. They just did not have enough staff and testing technicians to meet their schedule. Shortly after the *Enterprise's* arrival I was invited by the Commanding Officer to a luncheon at his quarters. The guest of honor was the Commander of Naval Air Forces Pacific Fleet (COMNAVAIRPAC). The Vice Admiral was very concerned that the shipyard would meet the eighteen month schedule because he had a limited number of carriers and any delay would impact his ability to meet the Navy's commitments in the Pacific. Each of the shipyard managers attending the luncheon assured him that they would meet the schedule. Finally the Vice Admiral asked me what I thought. I explained the difficulties with the current schedule and concluded by saying, "I would be extremely surprised if the work was completed in twenty-eight months." Needless to say he was shocked by my assessment and the Shipyard Commander forcefully restated that they would meet the eighteen month schedule. Unfortunately I was wrong and it took the shipyard thirty-six months not twenty-eight to complete the *Enterprise's* overhaul.

The shipyard would publish a new schedule at the last minute before each ship was leaving. Using the new schedule the shipyard could justify that they met this revised schedule, even though they were many months late in delivering the ship.

My retirement ceremony was held June 30, 1980, on board the USS *Missouri* (BB 63) at Bremerton, Washington. From there my wife, daughter, and I sailed away from Bremerton on my "dream sailboat," *Gryphon*. Leaving the U.S. Navy at this time was predicated by a "once in a lifetime" opportunity to sail with my family for a year and a half without any obligations. It also was the only way I could continue being "the Captain."

Finally I had to come ashore to meet a commitment I had made to my daughter that she could take her last three years of high school in a real school, not by correspondence courses. This led me to a second sixteen year career as a management consultant in the commercial nuclear power industry.

I retired again in 1997 and currently live in Solana Beach, California and Olympia, Washington.

CHAPTER X

Epilogue

Meeting Face to Face

In 1999 the U.S. submarine force began preparing for the celebration of the centennial anniversary in 2000. In order to produce a commemorative television program and publish a book documenting the development and accomplishments of the submarine force, a great deal of historical information had to be gathered. Although information was readily available documenting the development of the force and patrol reports detailing the exploits of our submarines in World Wars I and II, the operation reports of our submarines in the Cold War were all classified as Secret or Top Secret and, therefore, unavailable. In order to complete the story of the submarine force's hundred year history, the Navy decided to declassify two, out of hundreds of special operation patrol reports. These reports permitted a small part of the submarine force's Cold War exploits to be included in the centennial celebration. In June of 1999 my patrol report and the patrol report of the USS *Batfish* (SSN 681) were declassified. The declassification document is shown below.

DEPARTMENT OF THE NAVY
OFFICE OF THE CHIEF OF NAVAL OPERATIONS
2000 NAVY PENTAGON
WASHINGTON, D.C. 20350-2000

IN REPLY REFER TO
5510
Ser N87/9U657171
15 June 1999

MEMORANDUM FOR THE RECORD

Subj: DECLASSIFICATION OF DOCUMENTS

Ref: (a) EO 12958, "Classified National Security Information,"
          of 17 Apr 95

Encl: (1) USS Guardfish ltr 3840 Ser 00015-72 of 10 Jun 72
       (2) USS Batfish ltr LS-26-D-006-T-78 of 17 May 78

1. The Director, Submarine Warfare Division has conducted an
Original Classification Authority review and determined that
enclosures (1) and (2), as redacted, no longer require protection
under the provisions of reference (a). Accordingly, the
documents have been declassified and the appropriate stamps and
annotations have been affixed to render the material
unclassified.

M. I. FAGES
Director
Submarine Warfare Division

In 2000, a ninety minute television program titled *A Century of Silent Service* and a large, coffee table style book titled *United States Submarines* were launched by the Submarine Navy League to celebrate this centennial. The documentary, narrated by President Jimmy Carter, was broadcast on the History Channel. In preparation for this show, submarine Commander David R. Hinkle USN (Ret.) the Editor-in-Chief of Sonalysts, Inc. which produced the show and book, interviewed me for over an hour. Responding to interview questions from a speakerphone while being filmed and recorded was a first for me; the final portion was edited down to two minutes on the video and a generous four pages in the coffee table book. I laughed with my family that fame was fleeting.

Eight years later, in June 2008, I received an email identifying an internet site which contained an English translation of a Russian Naval blog. The narrative was written by Rear Admiral Alfred Semenovich

Berzin USSR (Ret.). As Captain First Rank he had commanded the Soviet Echo II (SSGN K 184), that *Guardfish* had trailed during the summer of 1972. When he received a copy of the book, *United States Submarines,* he immediately recognized the chart in my article *Guardfish Trails an Echo* even though he could not read English he realized his submarine had been the object of my trail.

His narrative in his internet blog included quotes from the account of the trail contained in the submarine book and observations from his personal diary. At that time I was considering writing a book about the trail. Now with Rear Admiral Berzin's account I hoped that we could combine our two stories into a really interesting book.[51]

Unfortunately contacting the admiral was not an easy task. Attempts through the internet and his blog address were unsuccessful. My step-daughter, Commander Christine McManus USN, volunteered to help and found that Rear Admiral Berzin had attended the International Submariners Association (ISA) conference in Russia. The ISA is a united cooperation of submarine associations of different participating nations. She was then able to contact a Mr. Lee Steele of that association and told him about me and my quest to correspond with Rear Admiral Berzin.

Mr. Steele did not have direct contact with the admiral but knew someone who did. In this roundabout fashion, we finally made contact. In February 2009 we started our personal relationship via email. In hundreds of emails we exchanged many of our memories of our lives, the Cold War, and of the trail. It was a fascinating discussion to hear the differences and similarities in our lives. From this discussion across the internet was born a deep and lasting friendship. Eventually my wife and I made the decision to journey to Russia to meet Admiral Berzin and his wife face to face.

In July 2012, my wife, Kay, and I started to plan our trip to Saint Petersburg; without her efforts we would never have been able to make this trip.

---

[51] Appendix D describes the difficulties in translating Russian text to English and the two Russian –American women who did the really hard work of interpreting Berzin's naval stories.

Rear Admiral Berzin and his wife, Penelope, spend most of the warm part of the year in their summer home twenty four miles north of Saint Petersburg. They return to their town home periodically during the summer for doctor appointments etc. and finally move home in October for the winter. October was chosen for our visit to coincide with this routine.

Having mentioned their summer home or dacha as they are called in Russia, I found Alfred's description of their summer home as a log cabin somewhat humorous. Alfred and his son-in-law Sergio built this cabin themselves years ago and it has been modified numerous times since then. This cabin is like no log cabin I had ever seen.

Rear Admiral Berzin described his summer home as follows:

"There are two stoves and a fireplace in my summer-house, I use birch firewood for heating, sometimes

electric heaters as well. We cook on an electric cooker,
there is also gas. Water supply is arranged from a one
hundred meter deep well. The water is very good qual-
ity and it's healthy. On the first floor there are three
rooms and a kitchen. On the second floor there is a
music center, library, and a huge dance hall. We have
satellite TV there. We also have a Russian style bath
in a separate building where we can wash and make
special Russian massages using birch brooms. Next to
our fence there is a forest where we gather mushroom
and hunt berries. The bus stop is nearby and it's only
fifty minutes by bus to the city metro station."

Traveling to Russia at that time required a special visa approved by the Russian government. It turned out to be a long and expensive process. Three months lead time was needed and an invitation letter from the hotel where we had made reservations within Russia had to be obtained. Therefore Kay had to get reservations at the Petro Palace hotel and flight reservations before we could apply for the visa. It is my understanding that Putin had this time consuming process stream-lined to increase the tourist trade to Russia.

In preparation for the visit I started looking for a suitable gift for Alfred and Penelope. I looked at a number of possibilities; such as decorative glassware and antique nautical instruments. Nothing seemed to be right. I really wanted something which was represen-tative of the United States. I then thought of the silver Bicentennial Commemorative plate I had received from the wardroom officers of *George Washington*. Although I hated giving up this silver plate it was the perfect gift in that it commemorated our Declaration of Independence.

Along with the plate I provided the following description of the plate in English and Russian so that Alfred and Penelope could understand its significance.

GIFT FOR ALFRED AND PENELOPE BERZIN FROM KAY AND DAVE MINTON

The United States of America is a young country when compared with the rich history of Russia, but America was also born in revolution and war. This plate celebrates the bicentennial of the American Declaration of Independence on July 4, 1776. The center of the plate shows General George Washington crossing the Delaware River and contains the following quote by Thomas Paine.

"Those who expect to reap the blessings of free-dom must undergo the fatigue of supporting freedom."

The center picture is surrounded by the names of the original thirteen colonies and pictorials of the authors of the Declaration of Independence; John Hancock, Thomas Jefferson, Roger Sherman, Philip Livingston, Benjamin Franklin, and John Adams. Between the authors are copies of the signatures of all of the men who signed the Declaration.

General Washington accompanied by about two-thousand soldiers crossed the ice that jammed Delaware River by small boats on the night of December 25, 1776, in a surprise attack of the Hessian forces who were German mercenaries employed by British King George in Trenton, New Jersey. Only three Americans were killed and six wounded, while the Hessians lost twenty-two soldiers and ninety-eight injured. Americans captured 1,000 prisoners and seized muskets, powder, and artillery. This victory gave a huge boost to morale and was a turning point in our Revolutionary War.

Our last problem for the visit was to find a suitable translator. We had been given several names of translators in Saint Petersburg, but each one was either unavailable or hesitant to take the assignment. Finally luck stepped in. In passing Kay had told the Russian-American lady, Svetlana, who does her facials, about our search for a translator. Svetlana immediately contacted a friend she knew in Saint Petersburg and arranged for her to be available on October 5 and 6. This turned out to be a real gift. Emma Viktorovna was perfect and not only translated for us, but became our driver, tour guide, and good friend. We were ready to go!

The Berzin's had invited Kay and me to their home for dinner on the 5th and we had invited them into the city center for lunch on the 7th.

On October 4, 2012, we flew to Saint Petersburg and checked into our hotel room. With an eleven hour time difference our systems were way out of whack.

Our first meeting was on Saturday 5 October. Emma joined us in the hotel lobby at noon and whisked us away for a quick riding tour of the historic city center before going to the Berzin's flat for dinner.

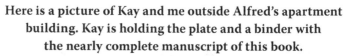

Here is a picture of Kay and me outside Alfred's apartment building. Kay is holding the plate and a binder with the nearly complete manuscript of this book.

After a quick greeting outside the building Alfred escorted us to his apartment. The following picture is of Kay and me and Penelope and Alfred. After several awkward moments getting the hang of using the translator we were introduced to their daughter, Ilona [52] and their granddaughter, Ana. Then Alfred and I made some opening remarks. In both cases we commented about what a wonderful occasion this was when two Cold War adversaries could meet as friends in peace. We then began to get comfortable with the translation process. I was pleased that Ilona knew some English and Ana was fluent in English.

---

[52] Ilona \i-lo-na\ is a girl's name pronounced eye-LONE-ah. It is of Hungarian and Greek origin, and the meaning of Ilona is "light", and is a variant of Helen. It is also carries the connotation of "beautiful" because of the beauty of Helen of Troy. The name of Ilona is mainly used in Hungary, Finland, and Latvia.

**Kay and I with Penelope and Alfred just after
we entered their dining room**

**The table before us was set with fine linens and really
beautiful china, crystal, and silverware.**

I then presented Alfred and Penelope our gift of the Bicentennial
Commemorative plate.

Alfred and Ilona looking at the plate.

Alfred, in turn, presented me with a beautiful ceramic plate showing Saint Isaac's Cathedral in the center surrounded by inserts of other historical sites in Saint Petersburg.

We then sat down to eat and exchange stories. Penelope, Ilona, Ana, and Kay were at one end of the table and Alfred and I were at the other end separated by Emma, the translator. This worked well in that Ana and her mother could translate for Kay and Penelope while Emma was helping Alfred and me.

Dinner had been specially made by Penelope. It was a Russian feast. It began with wine and toasts of welcome and for good health. The meal had many courses and was full of wonderful new tastes. The first course was appetizers and salads. Caviar on toast, smoked salmon, a special holiday family salad, Ana's favorite; cheeses and cold meats; sautéed chanterelle mushrooms picked in the forest near their dacha; fresh cucumbers and tomatoes; a beef gelatin salad. I am sure I must have forgotten some of the tasty items.

With all the talk I felt that I was lagging behind on eating. It tried hard to keep up, but every time I thought I was I was catching up Penelope would add something more to my plate. Finally we thought that we had come to the end of the feast — but oh no! After a short break to view Alfred's family photographs on his large computer screen, we had sautéed chicken and an unusual vegetable dish that Kay and I loved. A stack of zucchini rounds, onion, tomato and a mayonnaise cheese topping that was baked in the oven. Still more was to come – watermelon. And finally, tea and pastries, a lovely cake, and puffed dough rounds filled with whipped cream.

Somewhere during the meal Alfred had offered that I switch with him from wine to his favorite cognac. He explained that because of his type 2 diabetes he could only drink fifty-one grams at a time. After we both had several glasses of cognac it became apparent that this dinner was an exception to his limit.

Sea stories between Alfred and Dave with Emma translating

When Alfred started to tell one of his submarine stories I would respond that I knew what one. Ana was amazed that I knew or remembered all of them. I had to explain to her that I had read and reviewed each of his stories to be included in our book many times.

The process of creating her grandfather's sections of the book required many steps. First when I received a story from her grandfather in Russian then I used the computer to create a crude translation. Finding the story needed a lot more work I then sent it off to one of my

Russian-American translators to correct the computer's work. Because the translators could not fully understand the naval terms and the context of these stories it was now my job to interpret the story into more understandable English. As a result I had read and reread each story many many times.

I found myself very comfortable with Alfred. When I would ask him a question through Emma I could anticipate his answer from the sound of his voice and his body language. We had corresponded frequently for several years and really gotten to know each other. It was truly a great experience meeting Alfred and his family face to face. We discussed many things from religion to politics. I was surprised how much he and Penelope knew about our presidential election. They had been following it closely in the Russian news. They did not favor Romney because they thought he would continue to be anti-Russian.

During the course of the dinner and viewing their family pictures Penelope told us a little about her experience as a young girl during the Nazi siege of Leningrad (now Saint Petersburg) in World War II. She started by hugging a large piece of bread to her chest and telling us how much she loves Russian black bread and especially with butter. She considered it the most wonderful thing in the world ever since she suffered real hunger with her family during the siege.[53]

Although we had been at their home for six hours, eating, talking, and laughing it had passed very quickly. Kay and I were extremely honored to be invited to their home.

Tomorrow was Sunday and Emma was going to take us to see the historic city sights. Our next meeting with Alfred and Penelope was scheduled for lunch in the city center on Monday.

---

[53] The Siege of Leningrad lasted for a total of nine hundred days, from September 8, 1941 until January 27, 1944. The city's almost three million civilians (including about four hundred thousand children) refused to surrender and endured rapidly increasing hardships in the encircled city. Initially food and fuel stocks were limited to a mere one to two month supply. Public transport was not operational and by the winter of 1941–42 there was no heat, no water supply, almost no electricity and very very little food. At least 641,000 people died in Leningrad during the Siege, many of those by starvation.

Emma outside the Hermitage

We started the tour with the Hermitage. The building has an unbelievable collection of art, sculptures, and mosaics most of which had been stored away during the World War II siege of Saint Petersburg. Without Emma we would still be lost wandering around. The experts say that if you were to spend a minute looking at each exhibit on display in the Hermitage, you would need eleven years before you would have seen them all.

We then visited the Russian Museum which housed the work of Russian artists followed by a tour of several bridges crossing the River Neva. And we enjoyed the sights of the river and the great fort of Saint Peter which was built in 1703.

In old Russia the powerful Swedish Navy had controlled the Baltic Sea and each year when the ice in the Neva River melted the Swedish Navy would sail up the river and extract tribute from the city of Saint Petersburg. Emma told us an interesting story about the building of this fortress. Peter the Great was not pleased with this arrangement so when the Swedes withdrew for the winter he had a fortress built on Zayachii Ostrov, a small island in the Neva delta where two of the Neva's channels meet. The fortress was constructed in just two winter months. Even though it was not completed it was ready to defend the city when the Swedish Fleet returned in the spring. On seeing the fort, the Swedish fleet withdrew never to return again. Not one shot was fired. May 27, 1703, the day of this encounter, became the birthday of the city of Saint Petersburg.

Peter the Great did many wonderful things to establish the city. He designed the city's layout with broad streets. Even by today's standards they are wide and accommodate three lanes of traffic in both directions, green medians, and large sidewalks. Peter the Great unlike his predecessors traveled all over Europe and recruited many artists, musicians, and engineers to move to Saint Petersburg by offering them palaces, money, and nobility status. These newcomers help build the city into a "Venice of the North."

Peter the Great had planned that he would be buried in his Cathedral, but the Cathedral was not finished when he died. In fact it took eight more years before he was interred in his final resting place. In the interim he was laid to rest in one of his palaces. Emma was a great believer in the power of Peter the Great's spirit at this location and took us to the portico of his palace to see the giant Atlas statues which held up the portico roof. We were told if we touched a statue and asked for Peter's help we would get our wish. I wished that this book would get published soon.

Emma also took us to the Church of our Savior on the Spilled Blood. This marvelous Russian-style church was built on the spot where Emperor Alexander II was assassinated in March 1881 by a group of revolutionaries, who threw a bomb at his royal carriage.

On Monday it was our turn to entertain Alfred and Penelope for lunch. We chose a little restaurant near our hotel after checking it out for dinner Sunday night. The restaurant was on the second floor of what had been the palace home of Peter Ilyich Tchaikovsky, the famous Russian composer, and where he died on November 6, 1893. The food and service were very good and they had a large table in a small alcove just off of the dining room. It was a perfect location. While we waited, Emma picked them up from their home and drove them to the restaurant. Kay had selected several hors d'oeuvres to be served once they were seated. Without Ilona and Ana to help with translation I was concerned about our communications. I shouldn't have been concerned. Emma was able to handle several conversations at a time.

Kay talking to Alfred and Penelope.

**Alfred and I soon ordered some cognac and took
up where we had left off on Friday.**

Alfred came to our second meeting with a list of questions; such as, what did we generally eat for breakfast and lunch, what books had we been reading recently, and did we get together with our families on special occasions? He also asked Kay to write down our immediate family trees. He had seen pictures of all of our kids but wanted to make sure that he got them straight.

This lunch was really great and I had a hard time saying goodbye. Do Svidaniya (until we meet again) my good friend.

APPENDIX A

Biography of Captain David C. Minton III USN (Ret.)

David Minton was born in Leavenworth, Kansas on November 20, 1934.

PROFESSIONAL EDUCATION

In June 1952 he entered U.S. Naval Academy, Annapolis Maryland and graduated and was commissioned as an Ensign on June 1st, 1956.

In January 1959 Lieutenant Junior Grade Minton attended U.S. Naval Submarine School at New London, Connecticut.

In September 1960 Lieutenant Minton attended Nuclear Power School at Mare Island, Vallejo, California followed by six months training at the A1W reactor prototype in Idaho.

In November 1961 he took six weeks of S5W reactor systems training at the Westinghouse Bettis Plant near Pittsburgh, Pennsylvania.

In February 1968 he attended COMSUBPAC's Prospective Executive Officer School in Oahu, Hawaii.

In June 1970 Commander Minton was ordered to the USS *Guardfish* (SSN 612) via the Nuclear Reactor's (Admiral Rickover's) Prospective Commanding Officer Indoctrination Course in Washington, D.C.

SERVICE CAREER

In July 1956 Ensign Minton was assigned temporary duty to lead the USNA intercollegiate sailing team to the Academy's first National Championship win in Detroit, Michigan, after first participating in the Olympic Finn class sailing trials in Massachusetts.

In September 1956 Ensign Minton reported to USS *Bausell* (DD 845) stationed in San Diego, California, making two Western Pacific deployments.

In January 1958 Lieutenant Junior Grade Minton reported to USS *Gudgeon* (SS 567) in Hawaii making one Western Pacific deployment. He serving in *Gudgeon* for 1 1/2 years and finishing his submarine qualification.

In January 1962 Lieutenant Minton reported to the Blue Crew of the USS *Thomas Jefferson* (SSBN 618) in new construction at Newport News Shipyard, Virginia. On *Jefferson* he served in various engineering capacities through the construction period and made their initial Polaris.

Lieutenant Commander Minton then returned to Newport News Shipyard for a second new construction as Engineer Officer of USS *Sam Rayburn* (Gold) (SSBN 635). He served in that capacity through construction and two Polaris Patrols.

In June 1966 Lieutenant Commander Minton was assigned to Fleet Submarine Training Facility in Pearl Harbor, Hawaii, as Engineer Officer where he was in charge of the Engineering Training Department and during this short eighteen month tour he was instrumental in the construction of the first Submarine "Get Wet" Damage Control Trainer.

In April 1968 Commander Minton reported to the USS *Swordfish* (SSN 579) in Pearl Harbor, Hawaii, as Executive Officer and made two Western Pacific deployments.

In November 1970 Commander Minton took command of USS *Guardfish* (SSN 612) during her overhaul in Pascagoula, Mississippi. After transiting back to Pearl Harbor in 1971, Commander Minton took *Guardfish* on a Western Pacific patrol in 1972 that earned him the Distinguished Service Medal and the *Guardfish* was awarded the Navy Unit Commendation.

In March 1973 Commander Minton took command of USS *George Washington* (Gold) (SSBN 598) during their transit from Charleston, South Carolina, through the Panama Canal to the Pacific. *George Washington* was then homeported in Guam. Commander Minton made three Polaris patrols in *George Washington.*

After being relieved of command on June 28, 1975, he was assigned as the Readiness Officer for Submarine Squadron Three in San Diego, California, for two years.

For the last three years of his naval career he served as the Commander Submarine Force Pacific Fleet, Commander Air Forces Pacific Fleet, and Commander Surface Forces Pacific Fleet as their representative for nuclear overhauls at the U.S. Naval Shipyard Bremerton, Washington.

Captain Minton's retirement ceremony was held on June 30, 1980, on board the USS *Missouri* (BB 63) at Bremerton, Washington.

After retiring from the Navy he spent one and a half years living and cruising on his sailboat, *Gryphon,* with his wife and daughter.

In 1981 Captain Minton began a second career as a nuclear management consultant at the San Onofre Nuclear Power Plant in San Clemente, California. Except for several short breaks he worked there for the next fourteen years and then retired for good.

AWARDS

Breast Insignias
    Submarine Dolphins (gold)
    Command Pin
Polaris Patrol Pin (one silver and two gold stars)
Personal Awards
    Distinguished Service Medal
    Meritorious Service Medal (one gold star)
    Navy Commendation Medal
    Expert Pistol Medal

Campaign Awards
    National Defense Service Medal (one bronze star)
    Armed Forces Expeditionary Medal
    Vietnam Service Medal (three bronze stars)
    Republic of Vietnam Campaign Medal
    Sea Service Deployment Ribbon
Unit Awards
    Navy Unit Commendation
    Meritorious Unit Commendation

APPENDIX B

Biography of Rear Admiral Alfred Semenovich Berzin USSR (Ret)

Alfred Berzin was born on June 19, 1933, in the village of Krasnogorsk near Moscow.

PROFESSIONAL EDUCATION

In 1945 he was a pupil at Riga Nakhimov Naval (Marine) Academy in Riga, Latvia, and graduated in 1951.[54]

He then attended The 1st Higher Naval School of Submarines in Leningrad (St. Petersburg) as a cadet and graduated in 1955 with the specialty of "Officer Navigator of Underwater Swimming"(i.e., submerged operation of a submarine). In 1963 he graduated from the

---

[54] Nakhimov Naval School was created as a specialized men's secondary boarding school named after Admiral P.S. Nakhimov (1802 – 1855). The apprenticeship varied between four and eight years.

6th Higher Special Officer Classes Navy Fleet (command department) in Obninsk, with the specialty of a "Commander of a Submarine."[55]

In 1974 he attended a one year academic course at the Army Medical College.

SERVICE CAREER

From 1955 to 1957 he was a Commander of the steering group for Whiskey class diesel submarine SSG C 264 in the Baltic Fleet 135th Brigade, 27th Submarine Division attached to the Fourth Navy Fleet in Liepaja (Latvia).

From 1959 to 1960 he was at the disposal of the commander of submarine forces of the Baltic Fleet and made many trips abroad as ship's Navigator of the steam-ship *Vasily Kachalov*.

From 1960 to 1961 he was assigned as an Assistant Commander of the Whiskey class diesel submarine SSG C 163 in the Red Banner Baltic Fleet. From 1961 to 1962 he was assigned as Executive Officer of a Whiskey class diesel submarine SSG C 279 in the Red Banner Baltic Fleet in Ust-Dvinsk.

In 1962 he was transferred to the Pacific Fleet as an Assistant Commander of an Echo II class nuclear submarine SSGN K 56 and served in that capacity from 1962 to 1965.

From 1965 to 1969 he served as Executive Officer of an Echo II class nuclear submarine SSGN K 31 in the Pacific Fleet.

In 1969 he took command of an Echo II nuclear class submarine SSGN K 184 assigned to the 26th Division of Submarines in the Red Banner Pacific Fleet in Tihoakeansk.

In 1974 he was relieved of his command and placed at the disposal of the Main Navy Commander in Leningrad.

---

[55] Obninsk is a major Russian Science Center, located sixty-two miles southwest of Moscow. The first nuclear power plant in the world for the large-scale production of electricity opened there on June 27, 1954, and it also doubled as a training base for the crew of the Soviet Union's first nuclear submarine, the *Leninsky Komsomol*, or K 3. Now the city is home to twelve scientific research institutes. Their main activities are nuclear power engineering, radiation technology, medical radiology, and meteorology.

In 1976 he was assigned as the Chief of Staff and a Deputy Commander of the 26th Division of Pacific Fleet Submarines.

In 1976 he was assigned as a Deputy Commander of the 10th Division, Pacific Fleet Submarines.

From 1977 to 1982 he was assigned as Commander of 10th Division of submarines at the Pacific Fleet.

He received a military rank Rear Admiral after being a Commander of the 10th Division of Pacific Fleet for five years (a rare exception in the personnel policy of the Soviet Navy at that time).

From 1982 to 1988 he returned to Leningrad as head of the Department of Navy Tactics, 6th Higher Special Officer Classes Navy Fleet.

In 1988 he was discharged from naval service and retired in Leningrad.

From 1999 to 2007 he worked at a closed joint-stock company "The central company of financial-industrial group-Marine Technology as an Assistant Production General Director.

He is currently fully retired and lives in St. Petersburg.

AWARDS

Order of the Red Banner Third degree
Order for Service to the Homeland in the Armed Forces Third class
Medal for Impeccable Services Third class
Jubilee Medal Thirty Years of the Soviet Army & Navy
Jubilee Medal Fifty Years of the Armed Forces of the USSR
Medal for Impeccable Services First class
Medal for Impeccable Services Second class
Medal for Impeccable Services Third class
And several other medals

PAPERS

In the first issue of 1997 of the St. Petersburg magazine *The Captain -The Club* he published his memoirs under the title of *The Price of Error* dedicated to the submariners of Pacific Fleet, Rear

Admiral V.J. Korban, Rear Admiral Verenikina II, Captain First Rank G.A. Khvatova (when he was a commander of the submarine K 7) and to the other submariners.

In the ninth issue of 2000 almanac *Typhoon* he published an article *Swimming Under the Arctic Ice* dedicated to a meeting of the Nuclear Submarine SSGN K 320 (Nuclear multi-purpose submarine) in the Sea.

In the seventh issue of 2001 almanac *Typhoon* he published memories of the first patrol as commanding officer of the Pacific Fleet nuclear submarine, which was diving on the nuclear submarine SSGN K 7.

In the ninth issue of 2001 almanac *Typhoon* he published an analytical article entitled *The Human Factor* which was dedicated to the problems of the accidents in the Naval Fleet.

In his article *Cold War* about the military services of the Pacific Fleet nuclear submarines (26th Division) and about non-standard actions he took that prevented covert surveillance by U.S. submarines. This statement was confirmed by the release of a book in the USA, where U.S. commanders of submarines wrote about their common experiences with our submarines. In view of the fact that in the archives of the Soviet Naval Fleet such materials were destroyed, the unique experiences of our officers disappeared without a trace.

APPENDIX C

US and Soviet Naval Officer Titles and Ranks

In this book both Soviet Navy and U.S. Naval officer ranks are used and sometimes they can be confusing. The following is a table showing the two ranking systems.

U.S. Ranks	Soviet/Russian Ranks
Admiral of the Fleet (Wartime rank)	Admiral of the Fleet (Wartime rank)
Vice Admiral	Vice Admiral
Rear Admiral	Rear/Contra Admiral
Commodore	Captain First Rank
Captain	Captain Second Rank
Commander	Captain Third Rank
Lieutenant Commander	Captain Lieutenant
Lieutenant	Senior Lieutenant
Lieutenant Junior Grade	Lieutenant
Ensign	Junior Lieutenant
Chief Warrant officer	Chief Warrant officer/Midshipman
Warrant officer	Warrant officer/Midshipman

As you can see the Soviet Navy has four ranks that start with Captain. This causes some confusion but can be resolved by referring to their position, not their rank. Also any Soviet officer in charge of a ship, department, division, or combat unit is frequently called commander, even though there is no rank of commander in the Soviet Navy. Therefore in this book, chapters and stories translated from the Russian language to English, I use the officer's position or surname to identify the person. Officer ranks are only used when the person is identified by his full name.

U.S. naval officers also have confusing titles related to their position. For example the title Captain is used for the commanding officer of a ship, but his rank may not be a Captain. In the Cold War, U.S. submarine commanding officers were generally Commanders. The same is true of a Squadron Commander who was called Commodore even though he may just be a Captain. Although these ranks can be confusing, they will not detract from our stories and are listed here for clarification.

Soviet submarines were organized as follows:

Captain, Chief Officer, Political Officer, Mate; Departments and Service Organizations are headed by naval officers.

Each of the following five shipboard Departments is considered a combat unit:

- Navigation Department
- Missiles Department
- Torpedo Department
- Radio Department
- Electromechanical Department, with three divisions: Propulsion, Electrical, and Damage Control

The following shipboard Service Organizations are also headed by naval officers:

- Medical Service
- Supply Service
- Radar and Sonar Service
- Chemical Service

U.S. submarines were organized as follows:

Captain, Executive Officer, Departments, and Divisions are headed by naval officers.

The following are shipboard Departments:

- Operation Department (which includes: Operations Officer, the Radio Officer, Sonar Officer, and Electronic Material Officer)
- Navigation Department (which includes: The Navigator, the Quartermasters, and Navigation Electronic Technicians)
- Engineering Department (which includes: The Engineer Officer, the Main Steam Propulsion Officer, Reactor Control Officer, Electrical Officer who is responsible for the ships electrical equipment including the interior communications equipment, and the Damage Control Officer who is responsible for auxiliary equipment including the machinery to maintain the submarine atmosphere)
- Weapon Department (which includes: The Weapons Officer, Torpedo men /Missile Technicians, Fire Control Technicians, and Seamen)
- Supply Department (which includes: The Supply Officer, Storekeepers, and Cooks)
- Medical Department which generally consisted of a senior medical corpsman qualified for independent duty.

APPENDIX D

Russian Language Translation

The Russian text was translated by two women who grew up in the Soviet Union and are now U.S. citizens. Elena Sonina Smith who is working as a Russian Language instructor at the Evergreen State College and Natasha M. Hawkins a Registered Nurse working in cardiovascular surgery ICU at St. Mary's Hospital-Mayo Clinic. Both of these ladies did a wonderful job at the difficult task of translating texts which contained many naval terms and submarine jargon.

The other translation tool was the Google Translate program on the internet. While imperfect it allowed the authors to communicate with each other.

Major Russian Language Differences

The Russian verb "to be" is not used in the present tense (i.e., "am", "is" and "are"). For example if you were to say in English "I am a Russian;" in Russian you would say "I Russian." The Russian language does not have an equivalent for "the" or "a," so they must be assumed depending on the context. Pronoun objects like 'her' or 'it' come before the verb even if they are the object of the verb. Russians start a sentence with background information and build up to crucial information. For example if you were saying "There is no driver in the bus." Russians would say "In bus no driver."

An effort has been made to make the translated chapters read well in English without completely losing the flavor of the Russian language.

APPENDIX E

Relocation of nuclear submarines from the Soviet Northern Fleet to the Pacific Fleet from 1963 - 1968

Submarine Number	Project Number Class	Year of Transit	Dates of Transit	Submarine Commanding Officer	Senior Officer On Board [55]
K 115	627 A SSN November	1963	3-12 Sept.	Capt. 2nd Rank I.R. Dubyago	Capt.1st Rank V.G. Kichevo
K 178	658 SSBN Hotel	1963	14-30 Sept.	Capt. 1st Rank A.P. Michael	Capt. 1st Rank N.K. Ignatov
K 14	627 A SSN November	1966	30 Oct.- 7 Sept.	Capt. 1st Rank D.N. Golubev	Capt. 1st Rank N.K. Ignatov
K 42	627 A SSN November	1968	20 Oct.-5 Sept.	Capt. 1st Rank V.I. Zamora	Capt. 1st Rank A.P. Michael
K 55	658 SSBN Hotel	1968	25 Oct.- 6 Sept.	Capt. 2nd Rank Y.V. Peregoudov	Rear Admiral V.G. Kichevo

[56] In the Soviet Navy it was the practice to embark a Senior Officer to observe and assist the commanding officer, if necessary, during hazardous or complex operations including special operations. In the U.S. navy no Senior Officer ever accompanied the Captain on patrol.

From 1977 to 1980, five nuclear attack submarines, shown below, with cruise missiles of short-range, project 670, passed under the ice from the Northern Fleet to Kamchatka through the Arctic.[57]

Submarine Number Class	Year of Transit	Submarine Commanding Officer	Senior Officer On Board
K 429 SSGN Charlie 1	1977	Capt.1st Rank V.T. Kozlov	Rear Admiral E.D. Chernov
K 212 SSGN Charlie 1	1978	Capt. 2nd Rank A.A. Gusev	Rear Admiral R.A. Votes
K 325 SSGN Charlie 1	1978	Capt. 2nd Rank Lushin	Capt. 1st Rank E.A. Tomko
K 320 SSGN Charlie 1	1979	Capt. 2nd Rank V.T. Anikin	Rear Admiral E.D. Chernov
K 43 SSGN Charlie 1	1980	Capt. 2nd Rank N.Y. Maryashin	Rear Admiral B. Mochalov

---

[57] The Charlie 1 Class had eight SS-N-7 Starbright missiles with only a sixty kilometer range (thirty-seven miles).

APPENDIX F

Glossary

AN/BPS-9	Radar type used on Permit class submarines
AN/BQQ-2A	Passive sonar used to detect and analyze noise from submarines and ships
AN/BQR-20	Long range passive sonar used to detect and analyze low frequency noise from submarines and ships
AN/BQS-6A	Active search sonar that provides short to medium range and bearing to submerged or surface contacts
ASW	Anti-submarine warfare
Athwartship	A passage or beam running from one side of the ship to the other
AWOL	Absent without leave
Aysargi	A nationalist paramilitary unit that during the occupation of Latvia carried

out police and punitive functions ordered by the Nazi's.

Bathythermograph | An instrument that records water temperature in relation to ocean depth is frequently used by a submarine to determine the layer depth and evaluate the best depth to remain undetected

Battle Efficiency Award | Awarded annually to the best submarine in each U.S. submarine division

BT | Bathythermograph a device to measure water temperature

CIC | Combat Information Center

CINPACFLT | Commander in Chief U.S. Pacific Fleet

COMSEVENTHFLT | Commander for the U.S. Seventh Fleet (In charge of all naval forces in the Western Pacific as well as the forces operating off of Vietnam)

COMSUBFLOT SEVEN | Commander Submarine Flotilla Seven (In command of submarines deployed in the Western Pacific)

COMSUBPAC | Commander Submarine Forces U.S. Pacific Fleet

Critic Report | Early warning report of a significant deployment of Soviet naval vessels

DDC | Soviet Distance Disposal Container (Equivalent to our TDU)

DDR&E	Director of Defense Research and Engineering
DRT	Dead reckoning tracer used in the plotting table to project own ships movement from which the plotting team draws the bearings and calculates the range of the target
(dv)	Qualified Diver
ECM	Electronic Countermeasures
ESM	Soviet designation for electronic support measures
EM	Electrician's Mate
EN	Enginemen
ET	Electronic Technician
FTG	Fire Control Technician
Golden Anchor	Awarded for the highest enlisted retention rate in the Pacific Submarine Force
GPS	Worldwide global positioning system
HEN	HOTEL, ECHO, and NOVEMBER (first generation of Soviet nuclear submarines)
HF	High frequency
HN	Hospital corpsman

IDA-59	Individual isolation respiratory instrument enabling a submariner to breathe while leaving a sunken submarine
INPO	Institute of Nuclear Power Operations
ISA	International Submarine Association
MTR	Minimum trailing range, a distance considered necessary for safe trailing
Nasopharynx	Nasal part of the pharynx in the uppermost part of the pharynx extending from the base of the skull to the upper surface of the soft palate
NAVMAT	Office of the Chief of Naval Material
NAVSAT	Early navigational system using an orbiting satellite
Nestor	Device for encrypting voice communication
MM	Machinist's Mate
OPNAV	Chief of Naval Operations
ORESTES	Encrypted teletype communications device
ORSE	Operational Reactor Safeguards Examination
PCO	Prospective Commanding Officer

Polynya	Semi-permanent area of open water within a sea ice field or pack
PRF	Pulse repetition frequency
RCP	Russian Communist Party
RM	Radioman
Roadstead	Is a body of sheltered water outside a harbor where ships can be reasonably safe at anchor without dragging.
RPM	Revolutions per minute
RSDLP(b)	Russian Social Democratic Party (Bolshevik)
SINS	Submarine Inertial Navigation System
Spooks	Special Surveillance group
Sprint and drift	Technique used to regain contact by closing the range rapidly then slowing to search.
(SS)	Indicates a qualified submariner
SSBN	Nuclear Ballistic Missile Submarine
SSG	Diesel Guided Missile Submarine
SSGN	Nuclear Guided Missile Submarine
SSN	Stands for a nuclear attack boat. Sailors said it meant we work Saturdays, Sundays and Nights.

ST	Sonar Technician
STOPLIGHT	Soviet ESM antenna
STS	Sonar Technician, Submarine specialty
TASS	Russian government news agency
TDU	Trash Disposal Unit
TM	Torpedoman
UHF	Ultra high frequency
USSR	Union of Soviet Socialist Republics
WO	Warrant Officer
XO	Executive officer
Yankee Station	U.S. Naval War Zone along the Vietnamese coast
YN	Yeoman

APPENDIX G

Index

USS *Nautilus* (SSN 571)
   155, 171
USS *Queenfish* (SSN 651) 93
USS *Sam Rayburn* (SSBN 635)
   50, 208
USS *Swordfish* (SSN 579) 51,
   54, 58, 59, 60, 95, 208
USS *Thomas Jefferson* (SSBN
   618) 50, 208

V

Viktorovna, Emma 195
Vladivostok viii, xxii, xxiii, xxvi,
   104, 116, 136, 137
Vogt, Larry G. LCDR 100, 104,
   161, 233

W

Wilson, Harold K. ST1 (SS) 112,
   121, 122, 141, 165, 233

Y

Yokosuka, Japan 35, 58, 59, 95,
   123, 159

APPENDIX H

Awards

The following is a complete list of all *Guardfish* awards for this operation

CDR D. C. Minton, III, USN	Distinguished Service Medal
LCDR L. G. Vogt, USN	Legion of Merit
CWO2 F. R. Heckel, USN	Meritorious Service Medal
LT E. D. Bartel, USN	Navy Commendation Medal
LT R. C. Woodward, USN	Navy Commendation Medal
LTJG H. A. Williams, USN	Navy Commendation Medal
STC (SS) W. L. Treese, USN	Navy Commendation Medal
ST1 (SS) H. K. Wilson Jr., USN	Navy Commendation Medal
LCDR R. L. Graham, USN	Navy Achievement Medal
LCDR W. B. Byers, USN	Navy Achievement Medal
ST1 (SS) E. Y. Johnson, USN	Navy Achievement Medal
MM2 (SS) T. R. Lindberg, USN	Navy Achievement Medal
MM2 (SS) T. E. Cosgrove, USN	Navy Achievement Medal
LT A. J. Sisk, USN	ComSeventhFlt Commendation
LTJG G. R. Whaley, USN	ComSeventhFlt Commendation
LTJG L. G. Lewis, USN	ComSeventhFlt Commendation
LTJG M. Kovar, USN	ComSeventhFlt Commendation
MMC (SS) J.C. Seifert, USN	ComSeventhFlt Commendation
RMC (SS) A. O'Meally, USN	ComSeventhFlt Commendation

QM1 (SS) (Dv) C.F. Williams, USN	ComSeventhFlt Commendation
ETN2 (SS) C. E. Pilcher, USN	ComSeventhFlt Commendation
YN2 (SS) R.W. Sandberg, USN	ComSeventhFlt Commendation
IC1 (SS) R.C. Crespin, USN	ComSeventhFlt Commendation
WO1 D. B. Campbell, USN	ComSubPac Commendation
EMC (SS) A. D. Spencer, USN	ComSubPac Commendation
ENC (SS) B. A. Turner, USN	ComSubPac Commendation
IC1 (SS) D. G. Hackett, USN	ComSubPac Commendation
ST1 (SS) J. C. Scheldt, USN	ComSubPac Commendation
FTG1 (SS) S. K. Demrow, USN	ComSubPac Commendation
ET1 (SS) M. L. Jones, USN	ComSubPac Commendation
FTG2 (SS) D. L. Rummler, USN	ComSubPac Commendation
STS2 (SS) L. L. Kintner, USN	ComSubPac Commendation
STS2 (SS) H. J. Patterson, USN	ComSubPac Commendation
STS2 (SS) J. R. Becker, USN	ComSubPac Commendation
STS2 (SS) R. A. Veirs, USN	ComSubPac Commendation
ETR2 (SS) J. M. Lively, USN	ComSubPac Commendation
STS2 (SS) L. L. Torrison, USN	ComSubPac Commendation
STS2 (SS) R. S. Ashenfelter, USN	ComSubPac Commendation
ETN3 (SS) D. D. Sinclair, USN	ComSubPac Commendation
STS3 (SS) W. A. Peterson, USN	ComSubPac Commendation
IC3 (SU) W. V. Rogers, USN	ComSubPac Commendation

CPSIA information can be obtained
at www.ICGtesting.com
Printed in the USA
BVHW072302021220
594686BV00011B/239/J

9 781480 855533